GREYSTONE'S
Creative Hands

EDITOR

Beverley Hilton

GREYSTONE PRESS/NEW YORK · TORONTO · LONDON

# Volume 16

# Contents

© Fratelli Fabri Editore, Milan 1966, 1967
Marshall Cavendish Limited 1970, 1971, 1972, 1973, 1975
Manufactured in the United States of America
Library of Congress Catalog Card No. 75-8338

Much of the material contained herein has
previously been published in separate parts
under the title Golden Hands.

## The process and method

Tie-dye is the term given to a process where patterns are dyed into cloth, and it's so simple even a child can do it—and many children do produce beautiful examples.

The craft consists of taking a piece of fabric, then tying, folding, binding, knotting or sewing it so that when the fabric is dipped in a dyebath the color penetrates the untied areas and a pattern appears on the areas which have been protected from the dye. More complex patterns can be created by using more than one color, and retying first one area, then another. Tie-dye can be worked on lengths of fabric for home furnishings, on household linens or on garments. Dresses, blouses, skirts, pants, ties, pillowcases and curtains, can all be decorated with the tie-dye process.

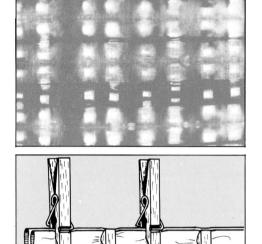

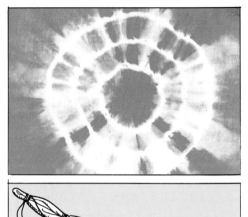

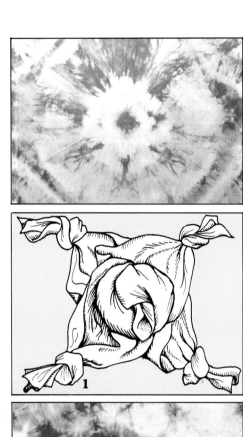

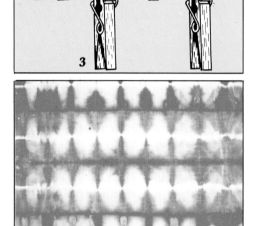

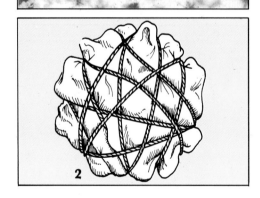

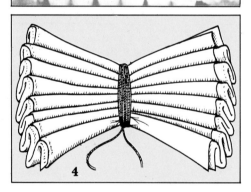

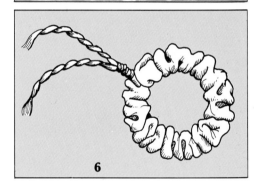

## How to make patterns

There are countless ways of tying up a bundle of fabric to produce a design. A picture guide is given in this chapter showing just a few of them and the patterns that will result.

**1.** Knotted squares. Pick up a point of fabric in the center of the square, knotting the point and each corner.

**2.** Marbling. Crumple up the fabric in the hand. Bind into a hard ball. Crumple in different places for each color used. For a large garment, bunch along the length, section by section, making a long firm roll.

**3.** Pleat a piece of fabric and secure with clothes pins.

**4.** Stripes. Fold a piece of fabric in four, pleat it and then bind with string.

**5.** Small circle. Pick up a piece of fabric to form a "furled umbrella" shape and bind with thread.

**6.** Ruching around cord. Roll a piece of cloth around a length of cord and ruch.

**7.** Clump-tying. **A.** Bind a cork into a piece of fabric.

**8.** Clump-tying. **B.** Tie a number of different sized stones into a piece of fabric.

**9.** Small circle. Pick up a piece of fabric to form a "flared umbrella" shape and cross

bind with thread.

**10.** Fold a piece of fabric in half and pleat it. Bind at various intervals with string, raffia and thread.

**11.** Twisting and coiling. Fold the cloth in half, pleat, then twist until it coils back on itself like a skein of yarn.

Bind at ends and at intervals.

**12.** Simple double knots.

Experiment and discover which pattern is the most suitable for the fabric or garment being dyed. Marbling makes a pretty, all-over pattern for most things and stripes are particularly effective on towels and curtains.

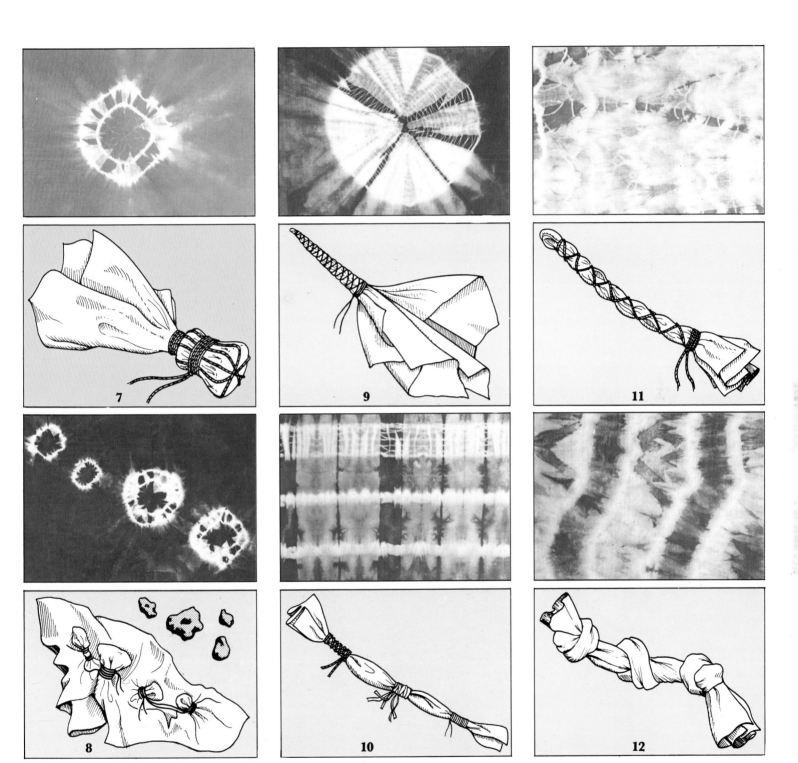

7

9

11

8

10

12

## Fabrics and equipment

Cold water dyes will dye natural fibers such as silk, cotton and linen in bright colors. They are easy to use and the results are wash- and light-fast. Cold water dyes come in a large range of shades, and one tin of dye is required for each $\frac{1}{2}$lb (250 grams) of dry fabric—i.e. two to three square yards of medium weight fabric. For example, a dress weighing one pound to be dyed blue and red will require two tins of each color. Some dyes are very concentrated and will dye larger quantities.

When fast color, cold water dyes are not available a hot water dye can be used, but the dyed garment should always be laundered separately. Hot dyes are also available in a wide range of colors, and will dye natural and some synthetic fabrics. Simmering will give the intensity of color intended, but the manufacturer's instructions for hot water dyeing should be followed exactly.

## Fabrics

It is not advisable to tie-dye woolen sweaters as the tying may make them go out of shape. Woolen fabrics can be dyed, but manufacturer's special instructions for dyeing wool should always be followed. Generally, cold dyes are a better choice for woolen fabrics than hot ones.

Fabrics unsuitable for dyeing are polyester/wool mixtures, acrylics (Orlon, Acrilan), and acetate rayon. Fabrics with special finishes resist dyeing and should not be chosen for tie-dyeing. Polyesters like Dacron, when dyed with triple strength hot dye in dark shades, will come out as pretty pastel shades.

Shirts, linens, towels and anything which is going to need constant washing should be dyed with a cold water dye, which is color fast.

## Other materials needed

☐ Salt
☐ Soda (for cold dyeing, not needed for hot dyeing)
☐ Wooden spoon to stir with
☐ Rubber gloves to protect hands
☐ Container, big enough to submerge the tied fabric; plastic or glass for cold water dye, a heat resistant container for hot dye
☐ Pitcher to hold one pint
☐ Thread, elastic bands, cork, pebbles, string, raffia, cord, cotton, or anything else needed to make the patterns.

## Hints and tips

• New fabric may have dressing in it which will resist dye, so boil the garment or fabric first, ironing it smooth again when it is dry.

• When making tie-dyed dresses, always tie-dye the material first, and then make the dress. The finished garment will have a much more professional look.

• Tie up a sample piece before immersing the whole piece of fabric in the dye bath. Dye, rinse, wash, and untie it, to see whether the resulting pattern and color is as required. Don't forget that the color will look darker when the fabric is wet.

• If an old, colored garment is to be tie-dyed to freshen it, remove the original color with color remover, but test a sample first to find out if the dye is fast.

• When two or more colors are used they will blend with one another, so choose color combinations carefully, remembering that red and blue make purple; red and yellow make orange; yellow and blue make green; and that a lot of colors mixed together will usually make mud!

## How to start

Bind the fabric in any of the ways shown in this chapter. Leave two inches of thread when starting binding, and when binding is completed return to the starting point and tie the two ends together. This will help to insure that the whole thing does not unravel in the dyebath.

If several bindings are being used on one garment, just use a slip knot and carry the thread onto the next binding.

For a sharp pattern, thoroughly wet the item before putting it in the dye bath. For a softer outline, put the item in the dye bath dry.

Prepare the dye. Always work the lightest color first.

For cold water dyes, dissolve the dye in one pint of warm water, stir well, and pour into the dye container. For each tin of dye used, dissolve 4 tablespoonsful of salt and one tablespoonful of common

▲ *An unusual way of using tie and dyed fabrics.* ▼ *Four neckties to make*

soda in one pint of hot water. Stir well, and when everything is ready to dye, add the salt and soda to the mixture. Once the soda is added to the dye, it is only effective for about two hours, so don't add until everything is ready. Otherwise, follow directions for your dye.

**Neckties from sheeting**
The four ties illustrated were made from tie-dyed cotton sheeting.

**Tortoiseshell banded tie.** Dye colors: coral red and café au lait.

Method: Fold a length of cloth 52 inches long by 7 inches wide in half along the length. Tie as many knots along the length as possible. Dye in coral red, rinse, untie, rinse again. Retie and dye in café au lait.

**Red ovals tie.** Dye colors: nasturtium and camellia.

Method: Fold length of cloth 52 inches by 7 inches lengthwise. Pick up small tufts of cloth along the fold and bind them narrowly, leaving a $\frac{1}{4}$ inch gap between each tie. Widen the tufts toward the end. Dye in nasturtium. After rinsing and while still tied, bind each tuft again below the original tie. Dye in camellia.

**Purple chevron tie.** Dye colors: French navy and camellia.

Method: Cut two pieces of cloth on the bias, each 28 inches by 8 inches. Fold each piece in half lengthwise. Roll the doubled cloth diagonally into a tube, beginning at the corners and working toward the folded edge. Make narrow bindings at 1 inch intervals along this tube. Dye each roll in French navy. Rinse, and while still wet, add further bindings between the original ties. Let the rolls dry and then dye again in weakly-made camellia colored dye ($\frac{1}{4}$ teaspoonful of dye made up to 1 pint with 2 teaspoonsful of salt and $\frac{1}{4}$ teaspoon of soda added).

Rinse well, hot wash and rinse again. Make a necktie by joining two pieces together and pointing the ends.

**Wide red tie.** Dye color: Camellia.
Method: Cut two lengths of cloth 52 inches by 6 inches. Fold in half lengthwise. Follow this procedure for both pieces. Pick up a piece of fabric, on the fold, about 4 inches from the end. Pull it into a tent shape and bind diagonally right up to the point, then back to the beginning and tie the thread ends. The tent shape by now should be a finger shape. Leave little gaps in the binding so that as the dye partially penetrates a criss-cross texture is achieved. Each of these bindings will make a circle. Make as many circles as required, decreasing in size toward the center. Tie from the other end in the same way. Wet the cloth and dye.

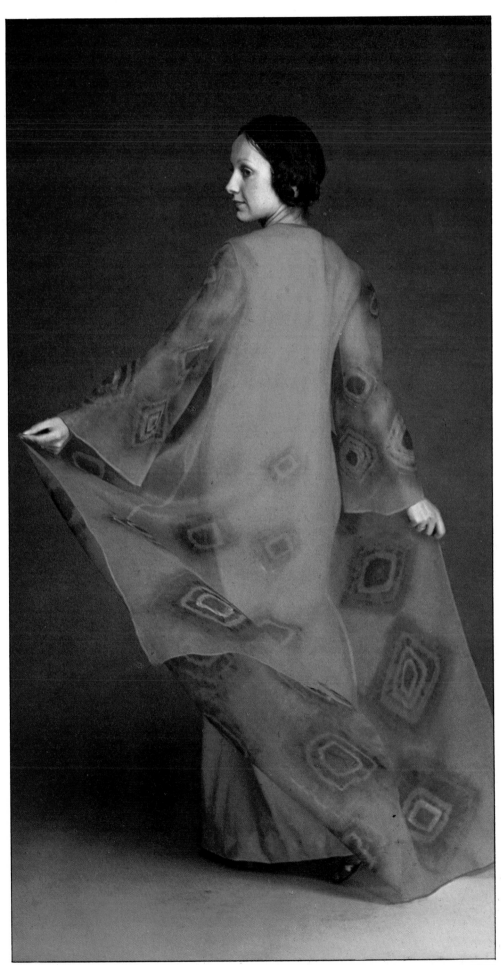

# Tailoring two

## A. About basting

Always work on a flat surface when basting* seams, details and canvases. This insures that the grain is kept correctly aligned and not pulled out of shape.

### Seams and details

**1.** Lay the pieces flat, right sides together, notches and balance marks matching exactly. Pin at right angles to the stitching line.
Using double thread, baste together, starting with a tailor's knot* and finishing with a backstitch.

### Seams with ease*

**2a.** Lay the pieces together, right sides facing, with the one to be eased on top. Pin the notches and divide ease equally along the length.
**2b.** Push ease down with fingers and baste, taking a small section at a time.

### Back shoulder dart

In most cases it is better to ease in the back shoulder dart for a smoother line rather than stitch the dart. Exceptions are with linen, or fabric with a high man-made fiber content, because it is not easy to shrink these fibers.

### Overbasting

**3.** Overbasting is used when basting for a fitting to give a smooth line and a better indication of fit.

## B. The first fitting

### Preparing for the first fitting

Before any sewing is done the coat must be basted together, tried on to see that it fits, and the initial alterations made.
**4a.** On the back, baste the style seams and baste the canvas to the wrong side along the neck and armholes.
**4b.** On the front, baste the style seams and the canvas darts or seams, then baste the
1656

canvas to the wrong side.
Baste the sleeve seams.
**4c.** Baste the center back seam of the under-collar then baste the collar canvas to the wrong side of the under-collar.
**4d.** Overbaste the side and shoulder seams and the under-collar to the neck.
Baste the sleeves to the coat taking great care to spread the ease evenly at the sleeve head.

### Fitting points

A well fitted coat feels comfortable, adjusts naturally to the activities of the wearer, is becoming in line and amount of ease, and is consistent with the current fashion.
Five interrelated factors are to be looked for when fitting a coat.
☐ Ease: there should be ease for movement without the coat being too large.
☐ Line: all vertical seams should be at right angles to the ground unless they are fashion features designed to be otherwise. All horizontal lines—the bust, waist, hips—should be at right angles to the vertical lines.
☐ Grain: as for line.
☐ Set or fit: a garment which sets well sits on the figure without wrinkles or strain.
☐ Balance. pockets, belts, buttons, hems to be proportioned correctly for the individual figure.

### Correcting the faults

Put on the coat, right side out, over the appropriate clothing. Pin the center front lines together and then check the following points. It is better if you can get a friend to help you here.
☐ Is the coat sitting on the figure correctly (**5**)? Are the lower edges level, the center back and center front lines vertical?
☐ Are the style lines right for the figure—sometimes a line over the bust can be moved for better balance (**6**).
☐ Look for strain points shown by wrinkles (**7a**). Unbaste and let seams out till wrinkles have gone. Repin.
☐ If the coat is too big it will hang in folds (**7b**). Unbaste and repin.
☐ Turn up the hem and check buttonhole and pocket positions. Unless they are fashion features, pockets should be placed so that they are easy to use—the usual position is about 2 inches below the waist and between the center front and side seam. If your hip or stomach is rather large a pocket could be inserted in a seam to give a smoother line (see Creative Hands chapter 39, page 774).
☐ Check that the fold of the lapel lies smoothly and continues on the under-collar (**8a, b**). An adjustment to the top button

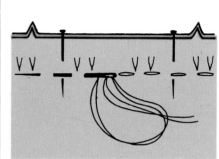
**1.** *Basting a straight seam*

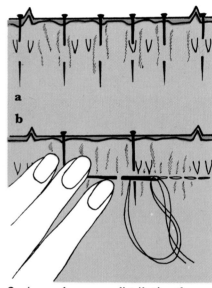
**2.** *An eased seam:* **a.** *distributing the ease;* **b.** *pushing in the ease and basting*

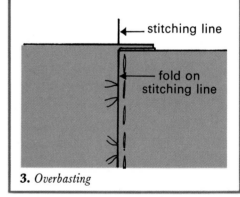
**3.** *Overbasting*

position can correct a loose or tight neckline (**8c**). An adjustment at the back neck seam may be necessary for a shawl collar to sit well.
Pin along the folds and thread mark when unbasted (**8a, b**).
☐ See that the sleeve hangs smoothly, that it is not too large or tight, and that the armhole line is well balanced. However, no alterations to the sleeve are made at this stage; the sleeves are put in to check the appearance and balance of the coat.

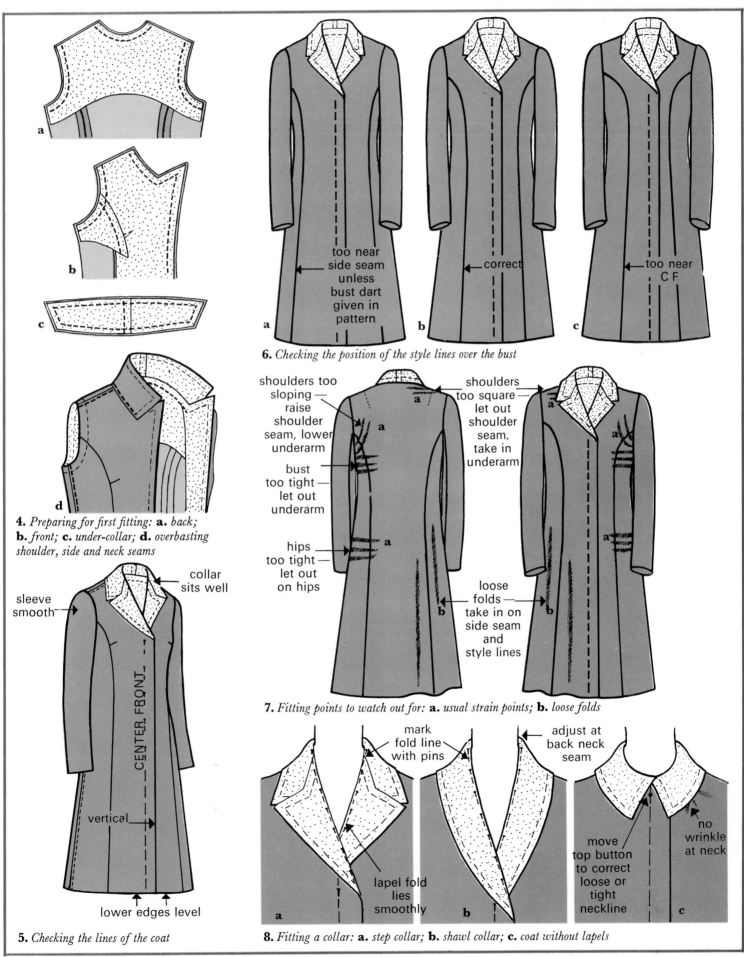

**4.** *Preparing for first fitting:* **a.** *back;*
**b.** *front;* **c.** *under-collar;* **d.** *overbasting*
*shoulder, side and neck seams*

collar sits well

sleeve smooth

CENTER FRONT

vertical

lower edges level

**5.** *Checking the lines of the coat*

a — too near side seam unless bust dart given in pattern

b — correct

c — too near C F

**6.** *Checking the position of the style lines over the bust*

shoulders too sloping — raise shoulder seam, lower underarm

bust too tight — let out underarm

hips too tight — let out on hips

shoulders too square — let out shoulder seam, take in underarm

loose folds — take in on side seam and style lines

**7.** *Fitting points to watch out for:* **a.** *usual strain points;* **b.** *loose folds*

mark fold line with pins

lapel fold lies smoothly

adjust at back neck seam

move top button to correct loose or tight neckline

no wrinkle at neck

**8.** *Fitting a collar:* **a.** *step collar;* **b.** *shawl collar;* **c.** *coat without lapels*

1657

## Pinning alterations

**9a, b.** To let out or take in a seam, first unbaste. Find the correct position for the seam then fold one side on the new stitching line and pin fold to new stitching line on under piece.

## Marking alterations

**10.** On shoulders and side seams thread mark any alterations in a new colored thread.

Mark through the fold and along the under piece.

Remove old markings.

**11.** On style seams slip baste* any alterations through fold and under piece. Remove old markings.

## Preparing to stitch

Unbaste sleeve, under collar, shoulder and side seams, but leave the style seams basted.

## C. About stitching

### Seams

**12.** To avoid damage to the fabric remove the tailor's tacks before stitching, and then stitch just outside the line of basting without catching it.

Seams with ease should be stitched with the ease side up as they are easier to control this way.

### Shoulder seams

**13.** Shoulder seams, however, are best hand sewn. For a firm result use a double silk thread and a backstitch. By doing this the ease is controlled, resulting in a straight line.

**14.** Before a seam is pressed the basting is removed and the edges made neat by overcasting in matching silk thread.

### Topstitching

Topstitching gives a professional finish when done carefully, so practice on a piece of fabric folded to the appropriate thickness.

Work the topstitching as the garment is being made, not when it is finished.

For topstitching work as follows:

☐ Set the machine to a large stitch.

☐ Use a number 16 (or 100) needle.

☐ If possible use buttonhole twist in both bottom and top of the machine. If you find this does not work try threading the top only with buttonhole twist.

☐ Check bobbin and refill if low.

☐ Baste just inside the topstitching line (**15**). Then stitch slowly and carefully, using basting, seam and machine foot as guide lines. When turning corners leave the needle in the work and pivot cloth on needle.

1658

## D. Pressing

To insure a smoothly finished garment each stage of the work should be pressed as it is finished. This needs care and plenty of patience.

Remember that pressing is not ironing and that the iron should be lifted and pressed upon the part required—not smoothed back and forth.

**16.** The positioning of the garment or part to be pressed is important and you should work in the direction of the grain.

Always test for the correct iron temperature on a spare piece of fabric. If there are any artificial fibers in the cloth, regulate the heat to these to avoid destroying them.

### Using a tailor's clapper

Pressing cloths must be damp rather than wet to avoid spoiling the appearance of the fabric and leaving a rough-dry look.

**17.** As the iron is lifted after each pressing, quickly remove the damp cloth and hold the tailor's clapper firmly over the pressed section for some seconds. This action helps to set the seam or edge professionally, insuring a crisper fold or flatter surface.

Press and clap the folds of pleats, hems, seams, darts, pockets and edges as the construction of the garment proceeds.

### Pressing seams

**18.** Remove all basting and press the seam flat to blend the stitches.

**19.** Lay the seam over a pressing roll, making sure that the rest of the garment is well supported. Press open with the point of the iron as shown.

**20.** Look at the right side to make sure the seamline is flat before pressing with a damp cloth and clapping heavily on the wrong side.

### Pressing eased seams

Where a seam has been eased or fabric is to be molded the technique of shrinking* is used.

**21.** Lay the garment flat on an ironing board, right side down. Shrink away the ease with the point of the iron and a damp pressing cloth.

**22.** Open the seam, lay over a pressing roll and shrink the eased seam edge. While damp, stretch * the uneased edge.

Finally press and clap the seam.

### Pressing darts

**23a.** After stitching, cut along the fold of the dart, cutting as near to the point as possible.

**23b.** Lay the dart right side down over a ham and press and clap the dart open, checking for a smooth line.

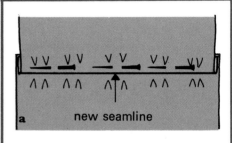

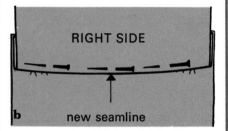

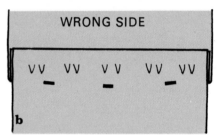

**9a, b.** *Letting out and taking in a seam*

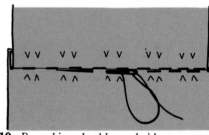

**10.** *Remarking shoulder and side seams*

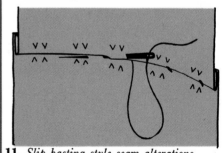

**11.** *Slip basting style seam alterations*

### Top pressing

Top pressing is used for lapels, collars and the final press.

Lay the garment on an ironing board right side up, smoothed into the correct position with the grain undistorted.

Cover with a piece of lightweight wool cloth. Over this, place the pressing cloth and press lightly. This prevents shine and removes any pin, basting or seam marks which might have been accidentally pressed in.

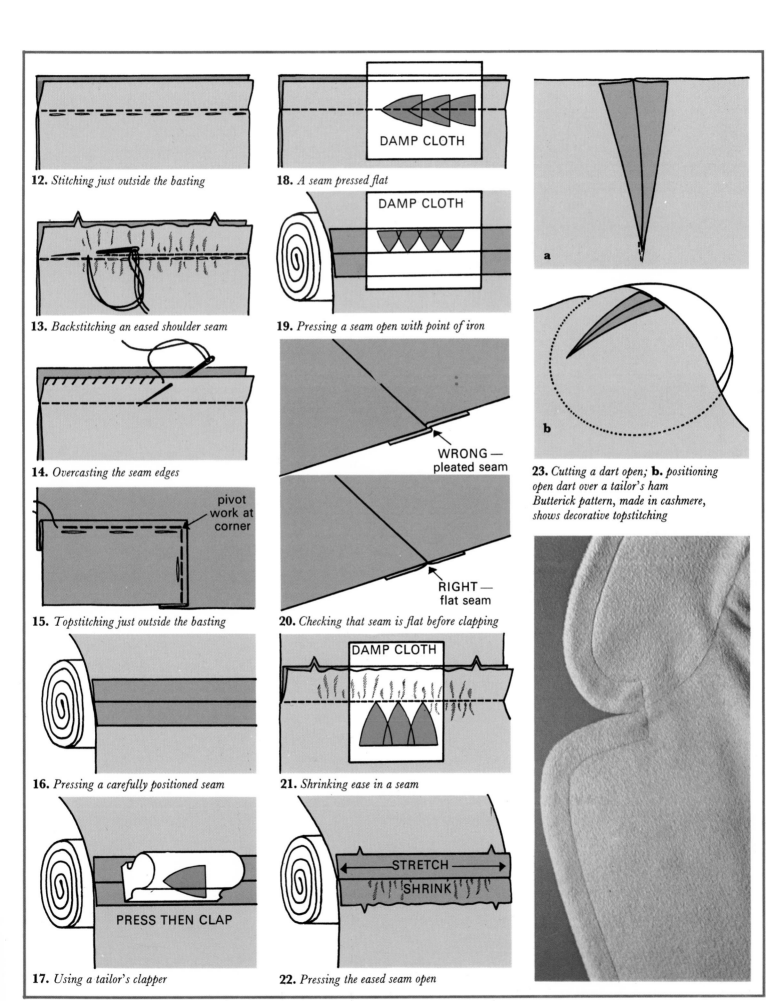

**12.** *Stitching just outside the basting*

**13.** *Backstitching an eased shoulder seam*

**14.** *Overcasting the seam edges*

pivot
work at
corner

**15.** *Topstitching just outside the basting*

**16.** *Pressing a carefully positioned seam*

PRESS THEN CLAP

**17.** *Using a tailor's clapper*

DAMP CLOTH

**18.** *A seam pressed flat*

DAMP CLOTH

**19.** *Pressing a seam open with point of iron*

WRONG —
pleated seam

RIGHT —
flat seam

**20.** *Checking that seam is flat before clapping*

DAMP CLOTH

**21.** *Shrinking ease in a seam*

STRETCH
SHRINK

**22.** *Pressing the eased seam open*

**a**

**b**

**23.** *Cutting a dart open;* **b.** *positioning open dart over a tailor's ham Butterick pattern, made in cashmere, shows decorative topstitching*

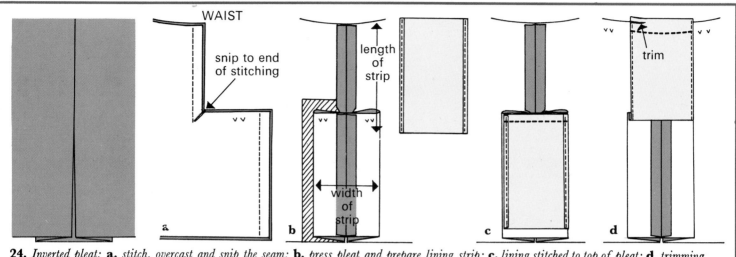

**24.** *Inverted pleat:* **a.** *stitch, overcast and snip the seam;* **b.** *press pleat and prepare lining strip;* **c.** *lining stitched to top of pleat;* **d.** *trimming top edge of lining strip*

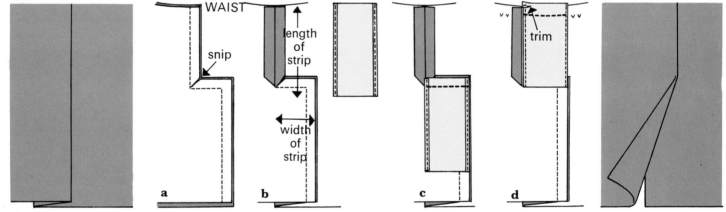

**25.** *Knife pleat:* **a.** *stitch, overcast and snip the seam;* **b.** *press seam and pleat and prepare lining strip;* **c.** *lining stitched to top of pleat;* **d.** *trimming top edge of lining*     **26.** *A back slit*

## E. Pleats

Because of the heavier fabrics used in tailoring all pleats need to be supported to prevent them from dragging and upsetting the balance of the garment.

### Inverted pleat

**24a.** Baste, fit, stitch, snip and make the seams neat. Press open.

**24b.** Put seams in line and press pleat, placing brown paper or cardboard under the fold to prevent marking the fabric.
Cut a strip of lining to the pleat width plus ½ inch, and to the length from the top stitching line of the pleat to the neck or waist.
Turn under each long edge for ¼ inch and stitch.

**24c.** Stitch this strip to each fold of the pleat.

**24d.** Fold up and stitch it to the coat just above the neck or waist seam. Trim to the curve.

### Knife pleat

**25a.** Baste, fit, stitch, snip and make the seams neat.

**25b.** Press the coat seam open and the pleat seam flat. Cut a strip of lining fabric to the pleat width plus ½ inch, and to the length from top stitching line of slit to the neck or waist. Turn under the long edges for ¼ inch and stitch.

**25c.** Stitch this strip to the top of the pleat.

**25d.** Fold up and stitch it to the coat just above the neck or waist seam. Trim to the curve.

### Slit opening (26)

Stitch as given for the slit opening in the pattern, then support as for knife pleat.

## *Terms and stitches

**Basting:** firm basting with ¼ inch stitches.
**Easing:** instead of a dart, shaping is obtained by easing one seam to another.
**Shrinking:** to shrink away the extra fullness which gives ease and to create shaping.
**Slip basting (27):** used to baste a seam from the right side after altering a seam (also used to match patterns, plaids, stripes etc). Fold top piece under on sewing line. Place fold over sewing line of lower piece. Sew taking a ½ inch stitch

through fold then a ½ inch stitch through under piece along the sewing line.

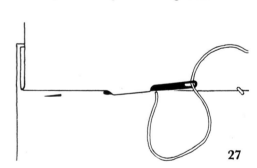

**27**

**Stretching:** to stretch fabric to make it lie flat as in curved seams, and to create shaping.

**Tailor's knot (28):**

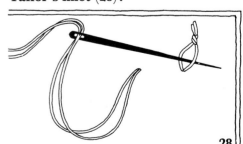

**28**

# Crafts/Making bead jewelry

## Beads in fashion

Decorative beads have played an important part in sophisticated fashion for centuries. Archeological finds in Egypt have uncovered ancient glass beads, beautifully shaped, and medieval women wore elaborate bead ornaments in their hair. Among the American Indians bead work was a major art, and their bold designs have influenced many contemporary fashions. In the nineteenth century, Victorian ladies made small beaded accessories as a home craft. Bead jewelry, or some

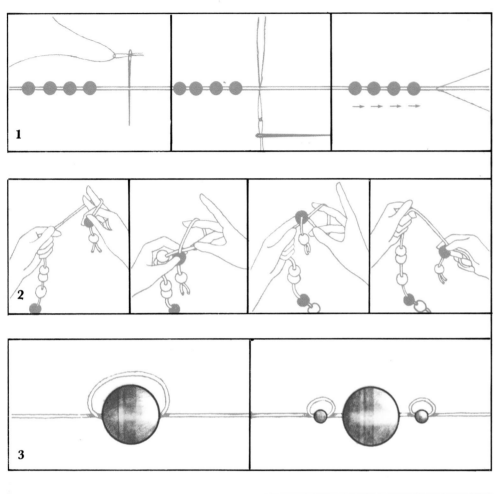

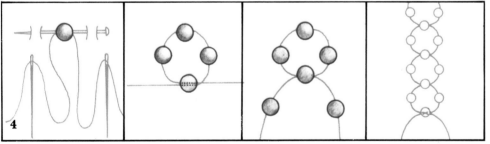

### Threading small beads
*Sometimes, small beads are sold strung on thread. If you break the thread the tiny beads spring apart. A useful tip is illustrated in diagram **1**. Thread a needle with cotton thread and pass the necklace thread through the loop of the cotton. Pierce the thread supporting the beads with the needle and pull the thread through. Hold the new bead thread parallel with the old and slide bead across.*

### Bead knotting
*When beads are to be spaced from each other either for appearance or for safety of precious stones, the simple knotting technique here is used. If thread seems too visible, a small bead is strung both sides of a large bead, the thread being strung through the small bead twice. On nylon, if small beads are threaded about 2 inches apart using this method, a pretty effect is achieved. Diagrams **2, 3◄▼***

### Jeweler's findings
*For some necklaces a metal clasp is needed for finishing and fastening. After a necklace or bracelet is finished, the thread ends are taken under the tongue and the back of the clasp and then taken up through the last two beads. Many different kinds of findings are available, some of them with perforated surfaces so that smaller beads can be stitched on. (Not illustrated.)*

### Two-thread technique
*This is the basic technique of beadwork and can be used with endless variations. Take a long thread and run it through a single bead. Push a pin through the bead and fix that to a cushion pad. Now working with both ends of the thread, thread a bead on the left-hand thread and another on the right-hand thread. Cross the threads through the fourth bead and proceed as before. Diagram **4 ◄***

---

form of decoration made from beads, has never been out of fashion for long, whether the feeling has been for the recent simple string of pearls or, by contrast, the heavy Victorian jet collars. Today, with current trends toward soft, informal clothes, beads are a natural accessory. In this chapter some, but by no means all, of the techniques of bead stringing are illustrated. The effects created can be as varied as the imagination and taste of the individual designer —from massive, sparkling necklaces to a single understated medallion on a leather thong.

Materials for beadwork can often be found just lying around, waiting for a sharp-eyed collector, although speciality shops can be an equally good source for discovering beautiful, expensive beads.

## Materials and equipment

### Beads
Almost anything through which a hole can be bored is usable as a bead: shells, seeds, fruit seeds, sweet smelling spices such as cloves and cardomom, nut shells, kernels, dried berries, animal and fish teeth, pieces of bone, scraps of leather, pieces of wood—all these have been successfully used for decorative jewelry.

More formal and familiar beads are usually either round, oval, square, raindrop or baton shaped and are made of precious and semiprecious stones, mineral substances, coral and jet, glass and crystal, porcelain, pottery, plastics and resins. Beads are obtainable in large or small quantities from craft shops, needlework shops and specialist suppliers.

Start a collection of beads for jewelry

making—it can be like searching for treasure. Chain store jewelry counters provide a variety of inexpensive bead necklaces which can be broken up and reassembled. Junk shops and secondhand clothing shops are worth searching for beautiful old beads which are now becoming scarce; and elderly lady friends can be counted on to have a broken bracelet or brooch tucked away. A single beautiful bead can be used as the centerpiece of a brooch and is well worth looking for.

### Threads and strings
A variety of different threads and strings can be used for making bead jewelry, depending on the design and the size of bead being used.

Bead silk, strong twist thread, any polyester thread, various weights of nylon thread, thin cords and wire are among

## Bead mosaic

*The diagrams here show how close, dense surfaces are built up. A row of beads is strung fairly loosely and then the thread is taken back through the last bead but one. A new bead is taken up each time, the thread going back through the second bead of the row before. This principle can be used with cord, nylon thread or wire. Pretty medallions, earrings and pendants can be made. Diagram 5 ►*

## Working with wire

*Working with wire, three-dimensional effects are possible. A pair of pliers is needed for this kind of bead work. The illustrations show how wire is bent into links for beads and how beads are secured by wire. For a dropping bead, for a pendant or an earring, a jeweler's pin is used. To hold a large bead securely at the end of a drop, the wire is threaded through a smaller bead. Diagrams 6, 7 ► ▼*

## Alternative finishing

*If a different kind of finishing is desired, the simplest is a bar and ring made of beads. Knot the threads through a bar bead and finish the ends through six beads making a circle. Glue the ends of the threads before passing them through the last bead. The glue will adhere to the inside of the bead and hold it securely out of sight. Use this method for finishing off thread ends (Not illustrated.)*

## Pendant earrings

*Here are some ideas for pendant earrings. A small, flat-backed bead is used to hide the metal finish of the earclip. Alternatively, glue a piece of fabric or leather to the clip and either cover it with beads or leave it plain. Wooden beads can be split to make half beads by tapping a tack into the hole. Paint them with shiny enamel paint or nail polish ►*

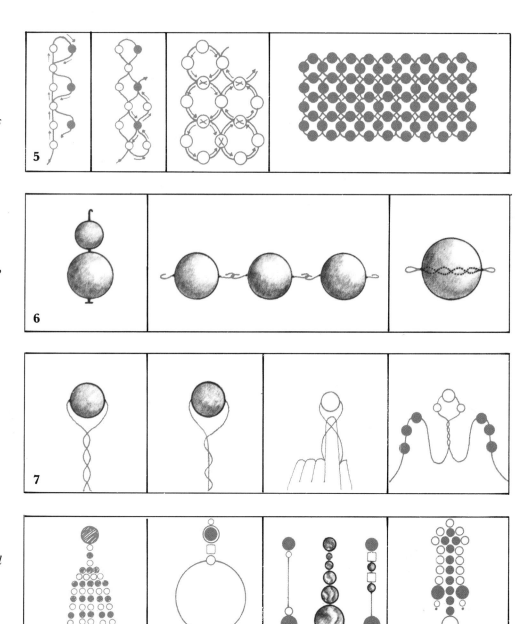

those most commonly used, but leather thongs, thick cords and macramé twine are also used for some types of jewelry. Dental floss, obtainable from most drug stores is also recommended.

Wire for jewelry making is available in soft copper, brass or silver. Copper plated steel wire is also used and is easy to work. Wire is available in a range of gauges. Florist's wire can be used for some techniques in jewelry making.

## Needles

Long thin beading needles are useful for threading beads with small holes, and needles of different gauges can be used as long as the eye will pass through the bead. Some threads are stiff enough to be passed through a bead without a needle, and other threads can be dipped in glue or twisted with soap to stiffen the ends.

For working with wire a pair of pointed, half-round pliers, a pair of side cutters for cutting wire, and a fine file are needed.

## Clasps and fastenings

Clasps and fastenings for jewelry are called "findings" and are obtainable from specialist suppliers and crafts shops in a wide and varied range of styles.

## Pins and working pad

For more intricate beadwork, such as mosaic beading, a working pad similar to that used in lacemaking is advised, a felt-covered brick or a piece of cork mat covered in felt will do. Long, glass headed pins are used for holding bead patterns in position during working.

A felt or velvet lined tray is ideal for making most other kinds of jewelry. The design can be laid out in the tray without

the beads rolling around, and if the fabric is of a dark color the color contrasts show up more clearly. A few small plastic pots near the work tray will conveniently hold beads while they are being worked.

## Techniques

Apart from the simple thread and knotting techniques used in single strand necklaces, there are other techniques in bead jewelry making which are more complex and require practice to perfect.

Mosaic beading, for instance, is rather similar to lacemaking and there are several variations on the basic patterns for achieving different effects. These are some of the techniques illustrated in this chapter and after awhile, you will be able to identify which have been used to produce this beautiful jewelry.

### for macramé necklace

☐ 4oz cone fine white macramé twine
☐ 24 long beads
☐ 20 round beads

### To make the necklace

Lay four lengths of twine together to form holding cords. Set on twenty-four doubled threads across the center of these holding cords.

Thread on beads as shown, working a square knot above the eight center beads and below all twelve beads. Thread on beads in the sequence illustrated, separating them with square knots and ending each column with an overhand knot.

Complete the neckband of the necklace by working square knots on either side of the beads to give the required length to fit around the neck.

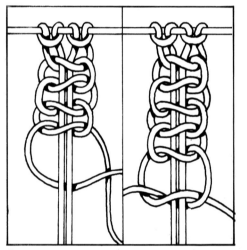

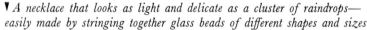

▼ *A necklace that looks as light and delicate as a cluster of raindrops— easily made by stringing together glass beads of different shapes and sizes*

▲ *A white macramé necklace with amber, red and white flat wooden beads*
▼ *Large and small beads strung closely together to make a solid necklace*

▲ *Different effects can be achieved using small colored beads or shells*
▼ *Eye-catching huge wooden beads look good strung on leather thongs*

▲ *Cord of different colors can be used as a contrast to the beads*
▼ *The variety of designs using toning and blending colors is endless*

# Knitting pattern/chunky jacket

The fastest thing on two pins is just the way to describe this long line cardigan. Worked on very large needles and using three strands of yarn simultaneously, it's fun to work and quick to complete. The result is a warm, richly textured cover-up to go with casual outfits when the temperature drops.

## Sizes

Directions are for 34in bust. The figures in brackets [ ] refer to the 36, 38 and 40in bust sizes respectively.
Length, 31[31:32½:32½]in.
Sleeve seam, 15½[16:16½:17]in.

### Gauge

6 sts and 9 rows to 4in over st st worked on Jumbo needles ¾in using 3 strands yarn tog.

## Materials

Bernat Krysta
18[19:20:21] 2 oz skeins
One pair Jumbo needles ¾ in
4 buttons

## Back

Using 3 strands yarn tog throughout, with Jumbo needles cast on 31[31:33:33] sts.
**1st row** K1, *P1, K1, rep from * to end.
**2nd row** P1, *K1, P1, rep from * to end.
Beg with a K row, continue in st st until work measures 8[8:9:9]in, ending with a P row.
K2 tog at each end of the next and following 6th row.
Continue without shaping until work measures 23[23:24: 24]in from beg, ending with a P row.

### Shape armholes

K2 tog at each end of next and every other row until 9 sts rem, ending with a P row. Bind off.

## Left front

Cast on 15[17:17:19] sts.
Work 2 rows in rib as given for Back, inc one st at end of last row. 16[18:18:20] sts.
1666

**Next row** K5[6:6:7], K into second st on left-hand needle then K first st on left-hand needle and slip both sts off tog—called TW2R —, placing needle behind first st on left-hand needle K into back of second st then K first st and slip both sts off tog—called TW2L —, K to end.
**Next row** K2, P to end.
Rep last 2 rows until work measures 11½[12:12:12½]in, ending with a WS row.
**Next row** K3[4:4:5], (P1, K1) twice, M1P, (K1, P1) twice, K to end.
**Next row** K2, P3[4:4:5], K1, (P1, K1) 4 times, P to end.
**Next row** K3[4:4:5], bind off 9 sts in rib, K to end.
With a separate length of yarn and a spare needle, cast on 8 sts. Work 3 rows st st, ending with a K row. Break off yarn.
Return to where main piece of work was left.
**Next row** K2, P3[4:4:5], P the 8 sts on spare needle, P to end.
Keeping the center 4 sts in patt as before, continue without shaping until work measures the same as Back to armholes, ending with a WS row.

### Shape armhole and front edge

**Next row** K2 tog, patt to last 4 sts, K2 tog, K2.
Continue dec in this way at front edge on every other row 4[6:5:7] times more, *at the same time* dec at armhole edge on every other row until 2 sts rem.
Continue on these 2 sts in garter st for 5in. Bind off.

## Right front

Work to correspond to left Front, reversing all shaping.

## Sleeves

Cast on 13[13:15:15] sts.
Work 2 rows in rib as on Back, inc one st in center of last row. 14[14:16:16] sts.
**Next row** K5[5:6:6], TW2R, TW2L, K to end.
**Next row** P to end.

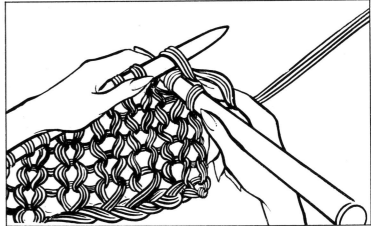

▲ *Showing the size of the Jumbo needles*
▼ *Close-up detail of TW2R which forms the cable-like panel*

Keeping patt correct in center, inc one st at each end of every 5th row until there are 22[22: 26:26] sts.
Continue without shaping until sleeve seam measures 15½:16:16½:17]in, ending with a P row.

### Shape cap

K2 tog at each end of next and every other row until 4[4:6:6] sts rem, ending with a P row.

Bind off.

## Finishing

Press work lightly under a damp cloth using a warm iron. Join raglan seams. Join side and sleeve seams. Join ends of Front bands and sew to Back neck. Make pocket linings from fabric and stitch in place. Sew on buttons using holes in knitting for buttonholes. Press seams.

1667

# Stitchery design/candlewicking

Candlewick originated in America in early Colonial days when, with a severe shortage of sewing materials of all kinds, women settlers used the thick cotton wick intended for candlemaking as an embroidery thread, working it into knotted and tufted designs on bedspreads. For many years the use of candlewick was restricted to bedspreads, but it looks effective in many other forms and can be used for pillows, rugs and bathmats as well as for warm garments such as bathrobes.

The tracing design given in this chapter is adaptable for almost any use and builds up well, placing the motifs as linking squares. It can be used for both tufted and smooth candlewicking and parts of the design could be adapted for a matching border motif.

### Materials for candlewick

There are two kinds of candlewicking, tufted and smooth, but for both types it is essential that the material on which the embroidery is worked should shrink on the first washing to secure the candlewick in the fabric.

Usually, bleached muslin is used for candlewick, but linen can also be used. It is important to choose a weave which will take two thicknesses of the candlewick cotton.

**Yarn.** Lily Mills Sugar'n Cream cotton can be used for candlewick and is sold in skeins or balls, available in a variety of colors. Skeins can be cut into 48 inch lengths or, if preferred, wound into a ball and used as required.

**Needles.** A special candlewick needle is used; this is large in size with a flattened, curved point and a big eye.

**Scissors.** It is essential to have scissors which are extremely sharp for cutting the loops. A blunt pair will drag and pull the tufts out of the fabric.

### Designs

Designs for candlewick are most effective when based on geometric shapes, but flowing designs can also be used if they are large sized. Small, intricate patterns are difficult to work and the shapes become distorted with the tufting. The candlewick can follow the outlines of the design, can fill in some areas, or cover the background completely as an all-over design, giving a solid area of pile texture.

### Tufted candlewick

In some early examples of candlewick, French knots and backstitch were used, but in modern embroidery the stitch mainly used is running stitch worked $\frac{1}{4}$ inch—$\frac{1}{2}$ inch apart along the line of the

▲ *A tracing design for working in either tufted or smooth candlewicking*

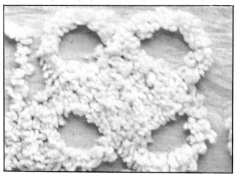 

▲ *A detail of the design above, enlarged and worked in tufted stitch and showing the reverse*

design, leaving a small loop between each stitch. To keep the loops of even length place a pencil under the cotton as each loop is made. The candlewick yarn is used double. Cut a length twice as long as is required and thread it through the needle until the ends are even. It is not necessary to finish off the ends when starting or finishing—begin on the right side of the fabric, leaving an end equal to the size of the completed tuft and end in the same way.

When all the design is completely worked cut the loops evenly with a very sharp pair of scissors.

### Smooth candlewick

This type of candlewick is worked simply in running stitch. One doubled length of cotton is used in the needle as for tufted candlewick and the stitches are worked about $\frac{1}{4}$ inch long and $\frac{1}{4}$ inch apart. This results in a bead-like stitch giving a beautifully raised, sculptured effect. This type of candlewick is at its best worked in geometric designs built up into solid shapes and covering the entire area of the fabric.

### Finishing candlewick

The completed work should be washed so

▲ *Smooth candlewicking in a modern bedspread*

that the fabric shrinks to fix the tufts more securely and to fluff them up. If a washing machine is used, wash for at least 20 minutes in warm soapy water. If washing by hand let the work soak for three to four hours. Do not wring or squeeze, just shake out.

Dry the work out of doors in a strong breeze and shake it frequently while drying to eliminate creasing and to make the tufts fluffier. Brush the tufts lightly with a soft brush before they are quite dry to fluff them up.

It is best to avoid ironing candlewick as this will flatten the tufts.

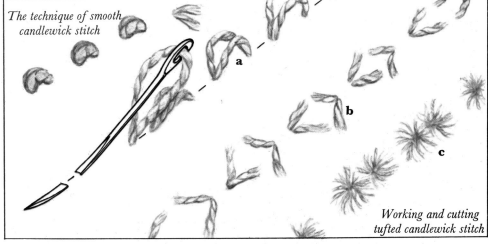

*The technique of smooth candlewick stitch*

a

b

c

*Working and cutting tufted candlewick stitch*

# Stitchery pattern/flower pillows, two charts

▲ *Floral designs worked on linen are fresh and colorful as a group of pillows or used individually*

The appeal of these pillows depends largely on the use of strong, clear colors to work the bold floral designs. Instructions and a tracing pattern are given here for each of the two pillows shown above right; the chapter beginning on page 1768 will include those for the two pillows on the left. These are just a few of a wide range of floral possibilities to be worked in the individual's choice of color and stitch.

To make each pillow measuring 15 inches square, you will need:
- ½yd 36 inch wide even-weave linen
- Sewing thread to match linen
- 10 inch zipper

- Pillow form 16 inches square
- D.M.C. 6-strand floss

## Peony pillow

You will need two skeins of D.M.C. 6-strand floss in each of the following colors:
**1.** Light blue 813; **2.** Medium blue 826; **3.** Light blue/lilac 334; **4.** Dark blue/lilac 336; **5.** Light lilac 209; **6.** Dark blue 939; **7.** Bright green 911; **8.** Dark green 890; **9.** Olive green 469.

### Method
This design is worked entirely in long and short stitch using two strands of thread in the needle. Commence working the

design from the center of the flower with the stitches lying in the direction indicated on the tracing pattern.

## Gypsophila pillow

You will need D.M.C. 6-strand floss in the following colors:
**1.** Light violet 334; **2.** Dark violet 312; **3.** Blue 826; **4.** Turquoise 519; **5.** Light green 955; **6.** Yellow/green 472; **7.** Dark green 905.
Two skeins each of colors 4, 6 and 7.
Three skeins each of colors 1, 2, 3 and 5.

### Method
Using two strands of thread in the needle,

*▲ A combination of stitches from the gypsophila*    *▼ Detail of peony reveals direction of stitches*

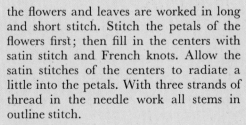

the flowers and leaves are worked in long and short stitch. Stitch the petals of the flowers first; then fill in the centers with satin stitch and French knots. Allow the satin stitches of the centers to radiate a little into the petals. With three strands of thread in the needle work all stems in outline stitch.

## Finishing

When all the embroidery is completed, press the work carefully on the wrong side. Make into a pillow measuring 15 inches square inserting a zipper centrally along one seam on the pillow. Press and insert pillow form.

**Tracing pattern for gypsophila**

1672

Tracing pattern
for peony

1673

# Costume design/19th century ladies

The main features of this costume from the 1880's are the high Empire waistline and the tubular dress skirt with its elaborate hem decoration. This was a graceful and feminine look and exceptionally flattering.

**The Dress**

The dress has a high waistline with a narrow waistband joining the skirt to the bodice. The skirt is gathered very slightly at the front and more fully at the back, standing away at the hem and finishing above the ankles.

Necklines of this period were either high and worn with puffed sleeves ending well below the wrist, or low with the puffed sleeves ending above the elbow. A frilled muslin neckerchief was worn to fill the low neckline. A Spencer was usually worn over the thin dress for warmth.

**Fabrics and colors**

Muslin, fine linen and cotton, embroidered or printed with dots, sprigs of flowers, and delicate border prints on white were most popular for day dresses, although soft pastel shades came in later in the period. For evening wear, gauze over colored silk or satin was fashionable. Outer garments were made from woolen or silk cloth; the Spencer was usually either blue or black.

**Accessories**

Bags of silk (bead embroidered or tubular knitted silk) were carried by ladies, and parasols, short gloves and small fans were necessary to complete an evening outfit.

Shoes were very pointed with tiny curved heels or no heels at all, worn with flesh or white colored stockings.

**Hats and hair**

Hats were richly trimmed; turbans, berets and tall crowned bonnets were adorned with frills, rosettes, ostrich feathers and ribbons etc. Mob caps which covered the hair and framed the face were worn indoors. Hair was centrally parted and arranged in curls on the temples with short ringlets and curls at the front and sides.

## 19th century costume

**You will need:**

**The dress.** 4 yards 36 inch wide material; cotton lawn, voile, muslin or any soft, light fabric, white, pastel or sprigged on white. Ribbons, flowers etc for decorating the hem.

**The Spencer.** 2 yards 36 inch wide coat-weight woolen cloth, blue or black.

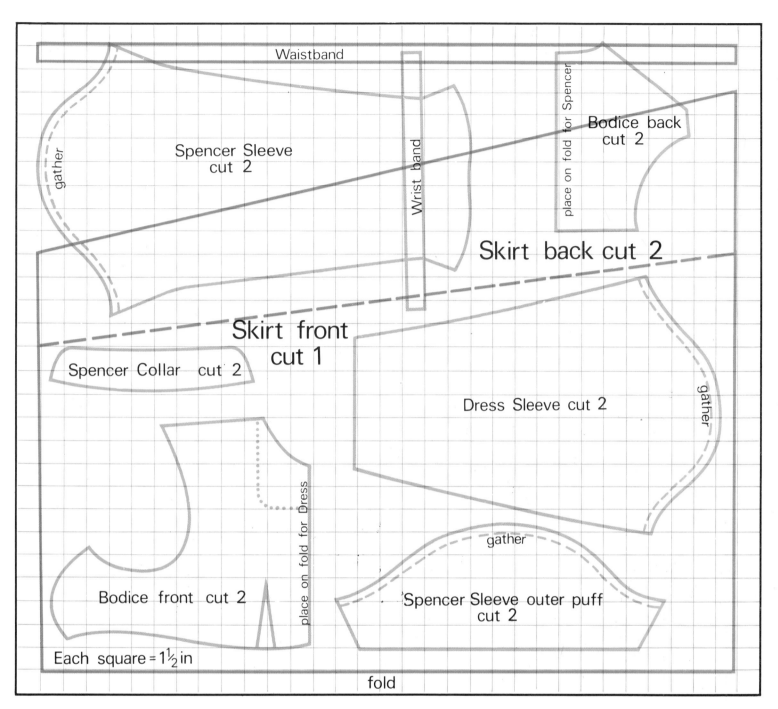

Waistband

Spencer Sleeve
cut 2

gather

Wrist band

place on fold for Spencer

Bodice back
cut 2

Skirt back cut 2

Skirt front
cut 1

Spencer Collar   cut 2

Dress Sleeve cut 2

gather

place on fold for Dress

gather

Bodice front   cut 2

Spencer Sleeve outer puff
cut 2

Each square = $1\frac{1}{2}$ in

fold

Matching braid.
(The graph pattern will fit 34 inch bust).

**To make the dress**
Make a paper pattern from the graph and separate the pieces of pattern.
Place the Skirt Front on the fabric folded lengthwise and cut out. Cut two Skirt Backs, without cutting on the fold, and join front to backs. Seam the center back leaving an opening 8 inches long at the waist.
Place Bodice Front on fold and cut out. Cut two Bodice Backs. Make the waist-bust darts on the bodice front. Join side seams and shoulder seams.
Leave center back open. Cut the Waistband on the straight of the fabric, to diaphragm measurement plus turnings. Sew to the bodice leaving the waist back open. Gather the waist edge of the skirt, gently at the front and more fully at the back. Join the skirt to the waistband, still

leaving the back of the bodice and skirt waist open.
Gather the top of the Sleeve pieces with running stitches. Sew the underarm seam, and pin the sleeves into position, the gathers at the top of the sleeve. Sew the sleeves in.
Face the neck, hem and cuffs. Sew concealed hooks and eyes down the back opening. Adjust the hem length and sew.

**To make the Spencer**
Cut out one Bodice Back, placing it on the fold of the fabric as indicated on the chart. Cut out two Bodice Fronts. Join the pieces on side and shoulder seams, leaving the front open. Face the front edges with self fabric.
Cut a strip 3 inches wide and long enough to fit the diaphragm measurement on the bias. Fold this to $1\frac{1}{2}$ inches wide and bind the waist edge of the Spencer.
Cut two collar sections in fabric and two

in interfacing. Make up the collar and attach to the neckline adjusting to fit comfortably. Sew hooks and eyes to close the Spencer front edge to edge.
To make the Spencer sleeves, cut out the outer puff section twice and the whole sleeve twice. Gather the top edge of the outer puff section with two rows of stitches and adjust to fit the armhole. Fasten off the thread. Sew the underarm seam. Sew a narrow hem along the puff edge cuff.
Stitch a strip of braid across the sleeve wrists of the main Spencer sleeves where indicated on the chart. Gather the top of the sleeve and adjust to fit the armhole. Sew the underarm seams. Finish off the cuff edge. Slip the puff over the main sleeve, pin both into the armhole and sew. To complete the look of the period, a roll is made by gathering a 10 inch long by 3 inch deep length of taffeta and stitching it to the inside back waist to lift the skirt.

# Tailoring three

## A. Canvassing the front and back

The canvas is sewn in place after any
style seams, darts and back seams have
been stitched but before the shoulder
seams and side seams are stitched.

### Padding the front canvas

After stitching the darts or seams on
the canvas (see Tailoring 1, D) trim off
the seam allowance plus $\frac{1}{16}$ inch on
the underarm, armhole and shoulder to
reduce bulk in seams.

**1a, b, c.** For a perfect result add a chest
pad of felt or loosely woven filler, stitched
to the canvas by staggered rows of pad
stitching\*. This does not add bulk but
gives a rounded line to the chest.
The padding is stitched to the side of the
canvas which faces the lining.

### Basting canvas to the front

Lay the canvas flat on a table, padded
side down. Over it lay the corresponding
coat front with the wrong side of the coat
fabric facing the canvas.
Match and pin the center and crease lines
together.
**2a, b.** Baste the following:
(i) Working from the bustline upward
baste the front edges of the coat to the
canvas, smoothing it up while working to
prevent wrinkles.
(ii) Repeat from the bustline downward.
(iii) Baste the opposite edge of the canvas
in a line from the hem through the bust up
to shoulder.
(iv) Baste around the armhole and along
the shoulder.
(v) Finally, baste along the crease line
of the lapel.

*A wrap-around coat and jacket in luxury
fabrics. The jacket, a Butterick pattern,
is made up in cashmere and features
raglan sleeves and a top-stitched step collar.
The coat, a Butterick pattern, is made up
in 100% angora with a Prince of Wales plaid.*

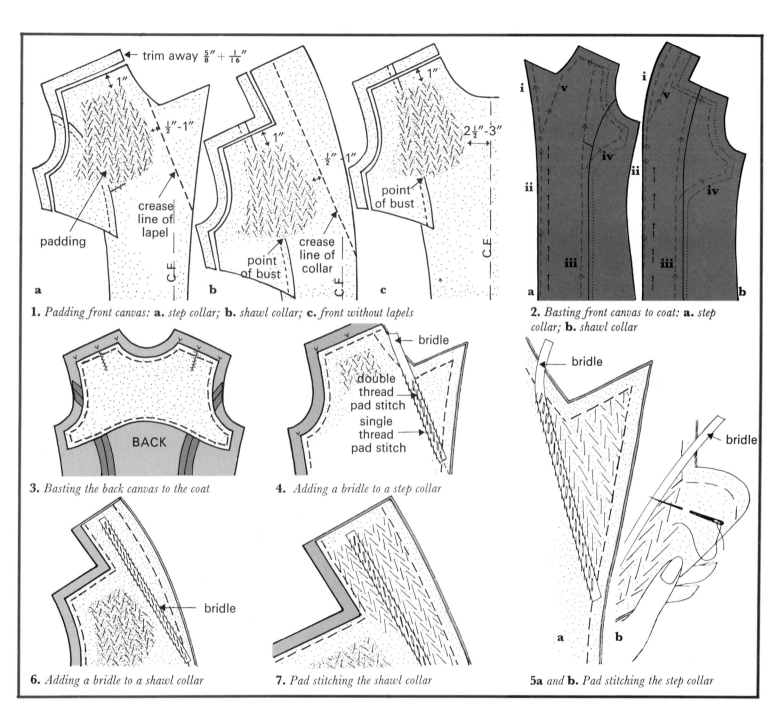

**1.** *Padding front canvas:* **a.** *step collar;* **b.** *shawl collar;* **c.** *front without lapels*

**2.** *Basting front canvas to coat:* **a.** *step collar;* **b.** *shawl collar*

**3.** *Basting the back canvas to the coat*

**4.** *Adding a bridle to a step collar*

**6.** *Adding a bridle to a shawl collar*

**7.** *Pad stitching the shawl collar*

**5a** *and* **b.** *Pad stitching the step collar*

### Basting canvas to the back

Trim off the seam allowance plus $\frac{1}{16}$ inch around underarm, armhole, shoulder and neck edges.

Stitch any darts or seams. Even if you have decided to dispense with the back shoulder dart and ease in the shoulder seam instead, you should make the dart on the canvas.

**3.** Baste canvas to the wrong side of the coat back as shown, easing the coat fabric to the canvas along the back shoulder seam if necessary.

### Adding a bridle

A bridle is a piece of $\frac{1}{2}$ inch wide linen tape sewn to the canvas along the roll line of a lapel, continuing into the step collar for 2 inches or to the center back for a shawl collar.

The linen tape should be shrunk by damp pressing or washing before application to prevent more shrinkage later.

**Step collar.** Cut a piece of tape to the length of the crease line plus 2 inches to extend into the collar.

**4.** Pin tape centrally along the crease line with 2 inches extending at the neck edge. Keep the tape taut.

Using a double, matching silk thread, pad stitch the tape in place along the center. This gives a strong central line. Then, with single silk thread, pad stitch along each edge.

**5a, b.** Starting from the bridle work rows of staggered pad stitching toward the edge. Keep the rows in line with the

bridle and don't sew beyond the seamline. Hold the lapel in a curled position with the left hand.

**Shawl collar.** Cut a piece of tape to the length of the crease line.

**6.** Pin tape centrally along the crease line keeping it taut. Using a double matching silk thread, pad stitch the tape in place along the center. Then, with single thread, pad stitch along each edge.

**7.** Starting from the bridle, work rows of pad stitching toward the edge. Shape the rows slightly at outer edge to allow the collar to set correctly, and don't sew beyond the seamline.

While working, roll the collar in a curled position with the left hand as for the step collar (**5b**).

### Front stay tape

**8a, b, c.** Stay tape is sewn to the front edges. On a coat with a step collar the tape extends from the hem to the top of the crease line (**a**) and on a coat with a shawl collar from hem to center back (**b**). On any other style the tape is taken up the front to the neck edge (**c**).

**9.** Before adding the stay tape, work as follows:

Trim the front edge of the canvas just within the sewing line to reduce bulk.

Cut linen tape to the required length.

Position the tape and baste the strip taut at the outer edge.

Catch stitch* the inner edge to the canvas.

### Finishing the canvassing

Finally, catch stitch the canvas to the coat at the underarm, shoulder and armhole on both back and front. Take care not to pull the stitches tight.

Working on the wrong side press well up to the crease line. Fold back along the crease line and allow the collar to roll, but do not press.

## B. Piped buttonholes

There are several ways of making fabric buttonholes. For the heavier weight fabrics used in tailoring the following method is very successful.

### Marking the buttonholes

The buttonhole length is the diameter of the button plus $\frac{1}{8}$ inch. If you buy the size of button suggested in the pattern then the buttonhole markings will be correct, otherwise, mark again, moving the inside tailor's tacks.

**10.** To insure that the buttonholes are in line and parallel to each other, prepare tram-lines on the markings, basting through both fabric and canvas. Remove the tailor's tacks.

### Making the buttonholes

For each buttonhole cut two pipes in the coat fabric. The pipes should be 1 inch wide and the length of the buttonhole plus $1\frac{1}{2}$ inches, cut in the straight grain of the fabric.

**11.** Position the pipes on the right side of the garment, with the edges meeting along the buttonhole line and right sides facing. Baste.

Chalk mark the ends of the buttonhole.

**12.** Working on the right side, stitch along the buttonhole length to each side of the buttonhole marking. The lines should be $\frac{1}{4}$ inch apart for buttonholes (and $\frac{1}{2}$ inch apart for pockets). At each end of the stitching over stitch for about $\frac{1}{2}$ inch to secure ends.

1678

Remove the tram-lines.

**13.** Working on the wrong side, cut along the buttonhole line making deep mitered v's at the corners at least $\frac{3}{8}$ inch deep. Take care not to cut the pipes.

**14.** Pull the pipes through the opening to the wrong side. Press the seams open, and the miters away from the buttonhole.

**15.** Working on the right side adjust the pipes into even folds and oversew to close. Stab stitch * along the seamline as shown.

**16.** At the back work an oversewing stitch at each end of the buttonhole to hold the facing in position.

**17.** Fold the garment back and backstitch through pipes and miter as near to the fold as possible.

## C. Pockets with lining

Pockets can be functional or decorative. The right place for them varies for each figure type, so make sure at the first fitting that they are in the right position for you.

### Interfacing a pocket

All pocket openings are interfaced with a strip of silesia, or duck, basted on the wrong side of the opening to support them.

**18.** Cut the interfacing with the grain falling along the line of the pocket where possible, and take it into a seam where practicable. Position and baste to the wrong side of the pocket opening, then make the pocket as follows.

### 19. Straight piped pocket

This type of pocket is attractive if made with contrast pipes. The average pocket length for a coat is $5\frac{1}{2}$ inches to 6 inches. For each pocket cut two pipes 2 inches wide and to the pocket length plus $1\frac{1}{2}$ inches, in the straight grain of the fabric. Make the pocket opening as for bound buttonholes (B), but with the stitching lines $\frac{1}{2}$ inch apart.

To finish, add the pocket backing and lining as shown in D.

### 20. Shaped piped pocket

Mark pocket position carefully with basting. Then interface the back.

**21.** To pipe the pocket cut a piece of fabric suitable for the pocket shape as shown, using coat or contrasting fabric. Position the piece of material, right sides facing, over the marked pocket opening, matching any design or check if appropriate.

Baste in place long pocket line.

**22.** Stitch carefully at equal distances from the basting. The width depends on how you would like the pocket to look.

**23.** Cut through patch only, as shown, to make pipes.

**24.** Cut through garment along pocket

*8. Stay tape stitched to front of coat with : **a**. step collar; **b**. shawl collar; **c**. coat without lapels*

opening, mitering corners.

Finish as for a straight piped pocket, snipping any curved seams.

Finally, add the pocket lining and backing as shown in **D**.

### 25. Piped flap pocket

Make a piped pocket without lining.

**26.** From the coat fabric cut a pocket flap to the length of the finished pocket and to the desired shape of flap, plus 1 inch on all edges for seam allowance.

Cut a lining for the flap to match.

**27.** Place pieces together, right sides facing, and stitch as shown. Snip across the corners.

**28.** Turn to the right side and press, then draw a chalk line 1 inch from the raw edge as shown.

**29.** Slip flap under top pipe and baste in place through all layers along the stitching line of the top pipe.

**30.** Turn to the wrong side and stitch in place over the original seam at the back of the top pipe.

To finish, add the pocket backing and lining as shown in **D**.

### 31. Flap pocket

Make the flap as for a piped flap pocket (figures **26**, **27** and **28**) and cut one pipe as for a straight piped pocket.

Interface the wrong side of the pocket opening.

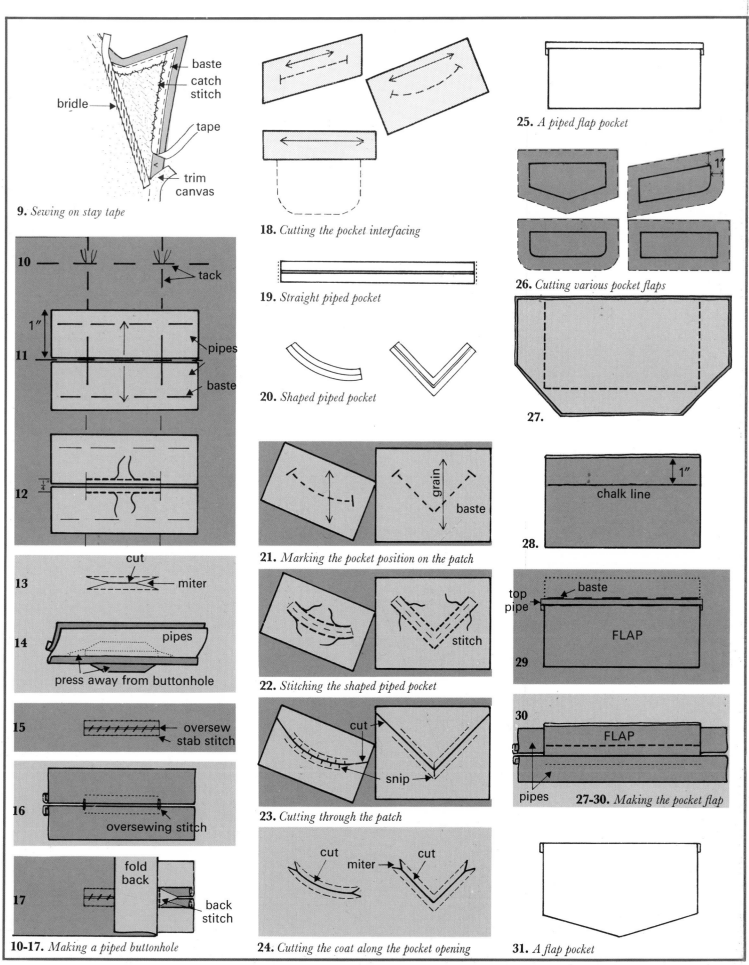

**9.** *Sewing on stay tape*

baste
catch stitch
bridle
tape
trim canvas

**10** tack

**11** 1" pipes
baste

**12** 1/4"

**13** cut — miter

**14** pipes
press away from buttonhole

**15** oversew
stab stitch

**16** oversewing stitch

**17** fold back
back stitch

**10-17.** *Making a piped buttonhole*

**18.** *Cutting the pocket interfacing*

**19.** *Straight piped pocket*

**20.** *Shaped piped pocket*

**21.** *Marking the pocket position on the patch*
grain
baste

**22.** *Stitching the shaped piped pocket*
stitch

**23.** *Cutting through the patch*
cut
snip

**24.** *Cutting the coat along the pocket opening*
cut
miter
cut

**25.** *A piped flap pocket*

**26.** *Cutting various pocket flaps*
1"

**27.**

**28.** chalk line
1"

**29.** top pipe
baste
FLAP

**30** FLAP
pipes

**27-30.** *Making the pocket flap*

**31.** *A flap pocket*

1679

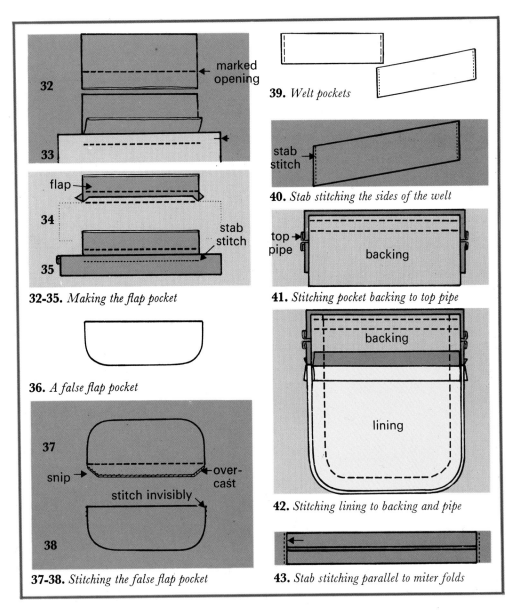

**32.** ← marked opening

**33.**

**34.** flap → ... stab stitch

**35.**

**32-35.** *Making the flap pocket*

**36.** *A false flap pocket*

**37.** snip → ... ← over-cast

stitch invisibly →

**38.**

**37-38.** *Stitching the false flap pocket*

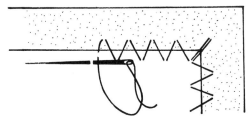

**39.** *Welt pockets*

stab stitch →

**40.** *Stab stitching the sides of the welt*

top pipe → backing

**41.** *Stitching pocket backing to top pipe*

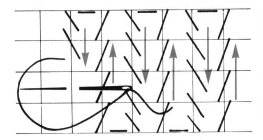

backing

lining

**42.** *Stitching lining to backing and pipe*

**43.** *Stab stitching parallel to miter folds*

---

**32.** Stitch the flap in place along the marked pocket opening, with right side facing.

**33.** Fold the flap seam up, out of the way, and stitch the bottom pipe in place as for a piped buttonhole.
Cut through the back of the opening as for a piped buttonhole.

**34.** Turn the flap seam allowance through the opening to the wrong side, leaving the flap on the right side. Press the flap seam allowance up and the miters away from the opening.

**35.** Pipe the lower seam opening as for a piped buttonhole.
To finish, add the pocket backing and lining as shown in step **D**.

**36. False flap pocket**
Make a flap as for a piped flap pocket. (figures **26**, **27** and **28**).
**37.** Position over opening and stitch. Cut away corners and overcast raw edge.
**38.** Press the flap down and fasten the

sides carefully.

**39. Welt pocket**
Make the welt as for the flap in figures **26**, **27** and **28**. Then make as for a flap pocket but placing the welt to the lower edge and piping to the top edge.
**40.** Finish the backing and lining as in **D**. Press the welt up and stab stitch* in place. If the coat is finished with top stitching you can topstitch the sides instead of stab stitching them.

## D. Lining a pocket

**41.** Cut a backing for the pocket in coat fabric, 3 inches deep and to the length of the pipe. Stitch to the top pipe or flap seam allowance as near as possible to the original stitching line. For added strength stitch again $\frac{1}{2}$ inch above first row.
**42.** For each pocket cut two pieces of lining fabric 4 inches deep and to the

length of the pipe. Stitch one piece of lining to the lower edge of the backing and the other piece to the bottom pipe or welt seam allowance.
Round off the lower edges of the lining as shown then stitch around to make the pocket.
**43.** Working on the right side stab stitch parallel to the miter folds for added strength.

## *Terms and stitches

**Catch stitch (44).** Used to catch one fabric to another where bulk is to be avoided. Lift one thread of fabric with each stitch so it will be invisible on right side. Do not pull stitches tight.

**Pad stitching (45).** Worked as shown, the needle to be at right angles to the stitching line. Work with an imaginary grid, coming down one line and going up the next, without turning the work. Stagger the stitches to prevent pleats being formed.
Use small stitches (about $\frac{1}{4}$-$\frac{1}{2}$ inch long) for stitching canvas to lapel and collar to create a roll.
Use medium stitches (about 1 inch long) for lashing padding to canvas.
Use large stitches (about 2 inches long) for quick basting.

**Stab stitch (46).** Used where almost invisible stitches are needed to hold fabric layers together firmly.
**a.** Working from the right side, push needle down vertically, pull needle through from wrong side.
**b.** Then push needle up vertically and pull through from right side.
The stitches should be very small.

# Crafts/weaving

## An introduction to weaving

Weaving is one of the oldest handcrafts known to man, yet the basic techniques have hardly changed since earliest times. It's a craft that almost anyone can master without difficulty, whatever his age—the rag weaving examples shown on this page were worked by children.

Weaving is basically a very simple craft requiring a frame to hold the threads taut so that other threads can be interlaced at right angles.

There are several different kinds of looms and weaving frames available in craft shops. Each of them is designed in a different way to enable the weaver to interlace the yarns in the easiest manner according to the type of fabric to be woven.

The simplest weaving structure is a frame cardboard, a piece of cardboard notched at opposite ends with the warp threads strung between them. This produces small pieces of fabric. At the other end of the scale, a beginner can learn to weave on a four-shaft loom with equal

▲ *Study this picture of the finished frame loom before starting to make it. You will get a clearer idea of the use of various parts*

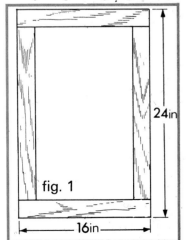

fig. 1

24in

16in

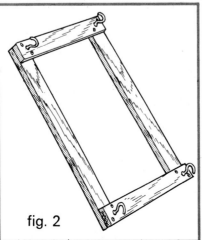

fig. 2

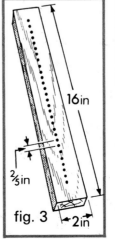

fig. 3

16in

$\frac{2}{5}$in

2in

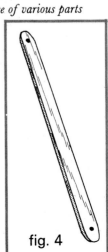

fig. 4

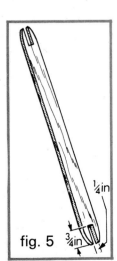

fig. 5

$\frac{1}{4}$in

$\frac{3}{4}$in

chances of success, and produce all kinds of woven fabrics for wall hangings, rugs, mats, table runners, clothes and accessories. As an introduction to this fascinating and absorbing craft, this chapter gives instructions for making a simple frame loom and setting it up for weaving, and suggests some ideas for using the woven fabric.

## Glossary of weaving terms

**Warp.** Threads stretched lengthwise on a loom.

**Weft.** The cross threads woven into the warp.

**Shed.** The wedge-shaped opening, created when alternate warp threads are raised or lowered; the space where the weft yarn travels across the warp.

**Raddle.** (Sometimes called the "reed"). A comb-like implement for separating the warp threads and "beating up" the weft.

**Leashes.** Strings tied to groups of warp threads, to pull them up to make a shed.

**Draft.** The way in which the loom is threaded up.

**Shed stick.** An implement which, when turned on its side, makes a shed for the weft threads to pass through.

**Weaving Stick (shuttle).** The implement upon which the weft yarn is wound, used to pass the weft threads through the sheds.

## A simple frame loom

To make the loom you will need:
☐ Planed lumber 10ft x 2in x 1in
☐ Planed lumber 4ft 6in x 1in x ¼in
☐ 3ft of ½in dowel rod
☐ 4 brass 1¼in hooks
☐ 8 1¼in No. 6 screws
☐ ½lb 2½in round head nails

### Constructing the frame
Cut the lumber into required sizes:
☐ 3 lengths 16 inches long and 2 lengths 24 inches long from the 2in x 1in lumber.
☐ 3 lengths 18 inches long from the 1in x ¼in lumber.

**Stage 1.** Place two 16 inch lengths across two 24 inch lengths to make a frame. Make sure the corners are absolutely square and screw the four pieces together,

using two screws on each corner (figure **1**).

**Stage 2.** Bore a hole in each corner of the frame between the screw heads, using a bradawl. Screw in the hooks so that the open end of the hook faces outward (figure **2**).

**Stage 3.** Cut the length of dowel rod in half. This is used to make the rods on which the warp threads are tied. The hooks hold the rods in position (see illustration of completed frame loom).

**The Raddle.** Draw a line down the center of the remaining 16 inch length of wood. Leaving approximately 1 inch at either end, mark points along the center line at ⅖ inch intervals. Drill ⅛ inch holes approximately ¼ inch deep at each point. Insert a nail in each hole and tap them home until they are firmly embedded. Do not hammer or the wood may split (figure **3**).

**Shed stick.** Take two of the 18 inch lengths of wood and drill an ⅛ inch hole at both ends of each piece, one inch in from the end. Round off and smooth the ends of both pieces (figure **4**).

**Weaving stick or wooden shuttle.** Using the remaining 18 inch length of wood, cut slots into each end 1 inch deep by ¼ inch wide as shown in figure **5**.

## Setting up the loom

### Putting on the warp
Cut warp threads twice the length of the weaving frame (48 inches) plus 10 inches and tie them onto one of the warp rods in the way shown in diagram A, making sure that the ends are of equal length. Space them evenly along the rod.

With a narrow end of the frame toward you, hook the rod into place at the far end of the frame and then tie the warp ends onto the front rod as follows: working from the center take a pair of warp threads and pull them taut over and under the front rod and tie in a single knot as shown in diagram B. This first knot will hold the warp rod in place at the front of the frame while you continue knotting all the warp threads. Make sure that the tension is even. When all the pairs of warp threads are tied, complete the knot as shown in diagram C.

The warp threads are now complete.

**Making the first shed.** Put the shed stick in position at the top of the frame by sliding it over the first right hand warp thread and under the first left warp thread and working thus across the loom (diagram D). Tie the shed stick with a piece of string through the end holes to prevent it falling out of the loom. When this stick is turned on its side it makes a shed for the weft threads to pass through.

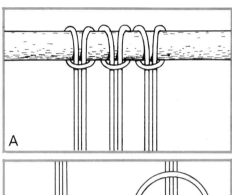

A

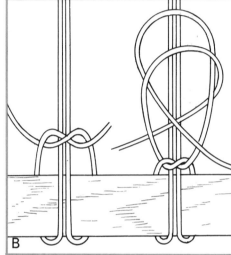

B

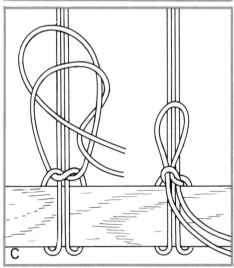

C

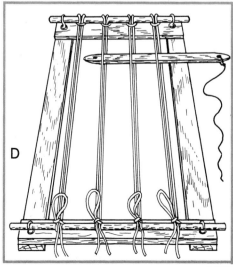

D

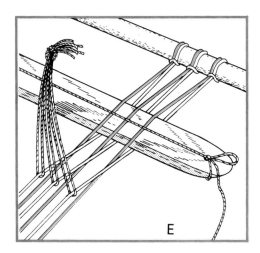

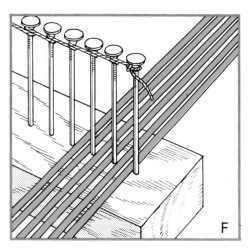

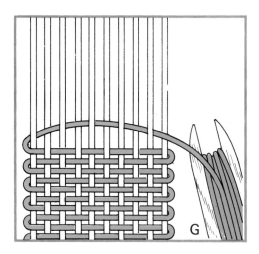

**Making the second shed.** The second shed is made using leashes and for these use a ball of soft firm string—rough string would damage the warp threads. Cut the required number of strings 18 inches long. Loop a piece of string under one of the right hand warp threads just in front of the shed stick. Knot the ends of the leash together evenly. Knot two more right hand warp threads and then knot the leashes together in groups of three about 4 inches above the warp threads (see diagram E). Tie the remaining leashes across the loom in the same way. The second shed is made by holding the grouped leashes firmly and lifting them so that the weft threads can pass through the space.

### Plain weave

To produce a plain weave, first one series of warp threads is lifted by turning the shed stick onto its side and then alternate threads are lifted on the groups of leashes. This means that (by counting from the right) the shed stick lifts even numbered warp threads and the leashes lift odd numbered warp threads.

### The raddle

The raddle spaces the warp threads evenly and is also used to beat the weft threads into position. Place the raddle on the loom in front of the leashes so that the warp threads go through the spaces between the nails in pairs. Then loop a piece of soft string around each nail to keep the warp ends from jumping out of position (see diagram F). The frame loom is now ready for the weaving to begin.

## Yarns

Because the frame loom has a fairly coarse construction, it is better to use a fairly thick yarn for the warp. Thick rug yarn or thick soft string would be suitable for the first attempt at weaving. Finer

yarns or mixed textures can be used when a little experience has been gained. It is important when choosing the warp yarn not to use anything that breaks or fluffs too easily.

Suitable weft yarns are cotton, wool, linen and string. For fun and more exciting effects try weaving with strips of paper, grass, rushes, cane, dried plants, lengths of beads, lace, ribbon, pieces of thin wood, or strips of colored fabric. Remember when using different yarns and colors to exaggerate the contrast to achieve the most interesting results.

## Starting to weave

Wind the weft yarn onto the weaving stick, making sure that it does not get too fat because it is then awkward to use. Turn the shed stick onto its side so that it makes a shed and slide the second shed stick through the space in front of the raddle. Holding the raddle parallel with the front of the frame, pull it firmly toward you until it can go no further. By putting the stick in at the beginning of the weaving you make sure that the warp ends lie evenly spaced for making an even textured cloth (see diagram G). You are now ready to begin using the weft yarn, which is passed through so that it lies in an arc on the warp threads and is then beaten evenly into position again at the front shed stick with the raddle. Lift the leashes and pass the weft through the shed. Begin and end weft threads in exactly the same way, by hooking the thread around the outside warp thread.

It is essential to keep the weaving the same width all the time and this is done by making sure that the weft threads are not pulled too tight. This is why the weft threads are left in an arc before being beaten into place and not pulled in a straight line across the cloth.

When the weaving is complete remove the leashes, the shed sticks and the raddle,

untie the half knots at one end and slide the rod from the other end.

### Finishing warp thread ends

For mats the ends of the cloth can either be hemmed and fringed or knotted and fringed.

### Weaves

On this draft plain weaves are woven but by free weaving (i.e. lifting the warp threads individually by hand and not using the shed stick and leashes) a greater variety of woven effects can be achieved. Free weaving is used when substances other than yarns are used for the weft.

## Things to make

### Shoulder bag

Weave brightly colored stripes of plain weave. Remove the work from the loom and sew up the sides. Fringe the warp ends to make an interesting border at the top of the bag. Add a cord for the handle and line the bag with a firm material. For a different effect, weave an inlay pattern on a plain background. Knot the warp ends together to form a side seam and sew up one side for the base of the bag. Add a handle and line with fabric.

### Mats

Make a set of mats in plain weave stripes, varying the combination of colors or textures for each mat. Fringe the edges. Rushes, canes, raffia, or string can be used for interesting textures but remember that the mats must be washable.

### Wall hangings

One can experiment and use different kinds of yarns and all kinds of objects to make wall hangings because they don't have to withstand wear and tear. If a great deal of color is required, keep the texture and weave simple. If rich texture is the aim, use very simple colors.

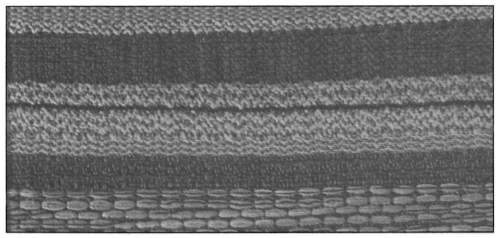

▲ *Fine jute warp, weft of mixed wool and worsted*    ▼ *Plain weave, 4 thin warp threads woven as one*

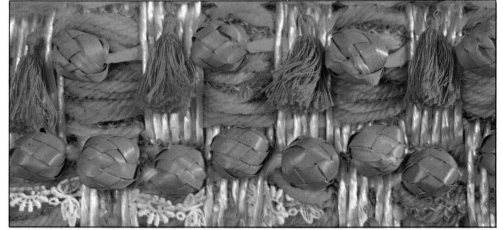

▲ *Plastic warp; lace, rayon tassels weft*    ▼ *Pattern here made by free darning on weaving*

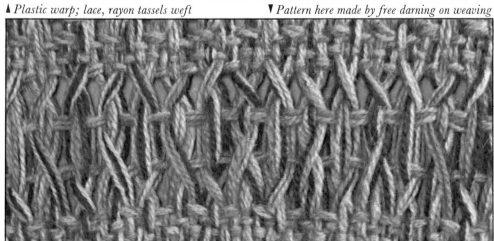

*Some of the things which can be made with the fabric woven on the frame loom*

# Crochet pattern/belted pants suit

This crochet suit is a useful addition to any wardrobe. The jacket has a heavily textured stitch which is repeated in a band around the pants hem. The remainder of the pants is worked in simple double crochet.

## Sizes

Directions are for 32in bust. The figures in brackets [ ] refer to the 35in bust size.
**Jacket.** Length, 27[27½]in. Sleeve seam, 15in.
**Pants.** Inside leg, 30in adjustable.

---

**Gauge**
10dc to 3in worked on No.G hook.
15 bean sts to 8in and 3 bean st rows to 2in.

---

## Materials

Bernat Berella 4 (Knitting Worsted)
8[9] 4 oz skeins
One No. G (4.50 mm) crochet hook
8 buttons
¾ yd elastic

## Pants left leg

Begin at waistline and using No.G hook, ch52[56].
**1st row** 1dc into 4th ch from hook, 1dc into each ch to end. 50[54] sts.
**2nd row** Ch3 to count as first dc, 1dc into each dc to end. Continue in dc, inc one st at each end of 5th and every following 5th row until there are 56[60] sts.
Continue without shaping until work measures 10in.

### Shape crotch

**Next row** Ch8, turn, 1dc into 4th ch from hook, 1dc into each of next 4ch, 1dc into each st to end, attach a separate length of yarn to the end of the row, ch5 and break off, then with original yarn work 1dc into each of 5ch. 67[71] sts.
Work 2 rows.
**Next row** Patt to within last st. Turn.
Rep the last row twice more. 64[68] sts.
1686

Continue without shaping until leg measures 27½in from beg of crotch shaping, or 2½in less than desired length.
**Next row** Ch3 to count as first hdc, 1hdc into next st, *(yoh, insert hook into next st and draw through loop, yoh and draw through 2 loops) 3 times into the same st, yoh and draw through all loops on hook—called bean st—, skip one st, rep from * to last 2 sts, 1hdc into each st. 30[32] bean sts with 2hdc at each end.
**Next row** Ch3 to count as first hdc, 1hdc into next st, 1 bean st into each bean st, 1hdc into each of last 2 sts.
Rep last row once more.
**Next row** Ch3 to count as first hdc, 1hdc into next st, 2hdc into each bean st, 1hdc into each of last 2 sts. Fasten off.

## Right leg

Work to correspond to left Leg, reversing shaping.

## Jacket back

Ch67[71].
**1st row** 1hdc into 3rd ch from hook, *skip 1ch, 1 bean st into next ch, rep from * to last 2 sts, 1hdc into each of last 2 sts. 31[33] bean sts with 2hdc at each end.
**2nd row** Ch3 to count as first hdc, 1hdc into next st, 1 bean st into each bean st, 1hdc into each of last 2 sts.
Rep the 2nd row until work measures 20in from beg or length desired to armhole.

### Shape armholes

**Next row** Ss over first 2hdc and first bean st, ch3, 1hdc into next bean st, patt to within last 2 bean sts, 2hdc into next bean st. Turn.
**Next row** Ch3 to count as first hdc, 1hdc into hdc, 1hdc into bean st, patt to within last bean st, 1hdc into bean st, 1hdc into each of last 2 sts.
**Next row** Ch3 to count as first hdc, yoh, insert hook into next st and draw through loop, insert hook into next st and draw through all 4 loops—

called dec 1—, patt to within last 3 sts, dec 1, 1hdc into last st. 25[27] bean sts with 2hdc at each end.
Continue without shaping until armholes measure 7[7½]in.

### Shape shoulders

**Next row** Ss over 2hdc and 3[4] bean sts, ch3, 1hdc into next bean st, 1 bean st into each of next 4 bean sts. Fasten off. Skip 9 bean sts in center, attach yarn, ch3, 1 bean st into each of next 4 bean sts, 2hdc into next bean st. Fasten off.

## Left front

Ch39[43] and work in patt as given for Back until work measures the same as Back to armholes. 17[19] bean sts.

### Shape armhole

**Next row** Ss over 2hdc and 1 bean st, ch3, 1hdc into next bean st, patt to end.
**Next row** Patt to within last bean st, 1hdc into bean st, 1hdc into each of last 2 sts.
**Next row** Ch3 to count as first hdc, dec 1, patt to end. 14[16] bean sts.
Continue without shaping until armhole measures 5in, ending at front edge.

### Shape neck

**Next row** Ss over 2hdc and 4[5] bean sts, ch3, 1hdc into next bean st, patt to end.
**Next row** Patt to within last bean st, 1hdc into bean st, 1hdc into each of last 2 sts.
**Next row** Ch3 to count as first hdc, dec 1, patt to end. 8[9] bean sts.
Continue without shaping until armhole measures the same as on Back, ending at armhole edge.

### Shape shoulder

**Next row** Ss over hdc and 3[4] bean sts, ch3, 1hdc into next bean st, patt to end.

## Right front

Work to correspond to left Front, reversing shaping.

## Sleeves

Ch41[45] and work in patt as given for Back for 10 rows. 18[20] bean sts.
**Next row** Ch3 to count as first hdc, 2hdc into the next st, patt to within last 2 sts, 2hdc into next st, 1hdc into last st.
Rep last row once more.
**Next row** Ch3 to count as first hdc, 1hdc into next st, 1 bean st into next st, patt to end, ending with 2hdc. 20[22] bean sts.
Work 3 rows without shaping.
Rep the inc rows once more. 22[24] bean sts.
Continue without shaping until work measures 15in from beg.

### Shape cap

**Next row** Ss over 2hdc and 1 bean st, ch3, 1hdc into next st, patt to within last 2 bean sts, 2hdc into next bean st. Turn.
**Next row** Ch3 to count as first hdc, 1hdc into next st, 1hdc into bean st, patt to within last bean st, 1hdc into bean st, 1hdc into each of last 2 sts.
**Next row** Ch3 to count as first hdc, dec 1, patt to within last 3 sts, dec 1, 1hdc into last st. Rep last 2 rows 2[3] times more. Fasten off.

## Collar

Join shoulder seams.
With WS facing, work 42[46] hdc around neck edge.
**Next row** Ch2 to count as first hdc, 1hdc into each st to end.
**Next row** Ch2 to count as first hdc, 1hdc into each of next 3[5]hdc, *2hdc into next st, 1hdc into each of next 2hdc, rep from * 11 times more, 1hdc into each of next 2[4]hdc. 54[58] sts.
Continue in hdc until collar measures 3in. Fasten off.

## Belt

Ch8.
**Next row** 1hdc into 3rd ch from hook, 1hdc into each ch to end.

Continue in hdc until work measures 30[32]in or desired length.

Dec one st at each end of every row until 3 sts rem. Fasten off.

## Finishing

Press pieces under a dry cloth using a cool iron.

**Pants.** Join Back and Front seams. Join leg seams.

Fold over first row at waist and slip stitch in place. Thread elastic through.

**Jacket.** Sew in sleeves. Join side and sleeve seams.

With RS facing, attach yarn at lower corner of right Front and work 1 row of hdc along front edge, around collar working 2hdc into each corner, then down left front edge, turn.

Mark position of 8 buttonholes on right front edge placing bottom one 2in from lower edge, top one just below neck edge, then 6 more evenly spaced between.

**Next row** Work in hdc to position of first buttonhole, (ch2, skip 2 sts, 1hdc to next buttonhole) 7 times, ch2, skip 2 sts, 1hdc in each st to end.

**Next row** Work in hdc with 2hdc into each ch2 sp.

Work 1 more row in hdc. Fasten off.

Work 1 row hdc around lower edge of jacket and sleeves.

Press all seams lightly. Sew on buttons. Sew buckle to straight end of belt.

*A stylish suit in simple crochet* ▶
▼ *Detail of bean stitch and double*

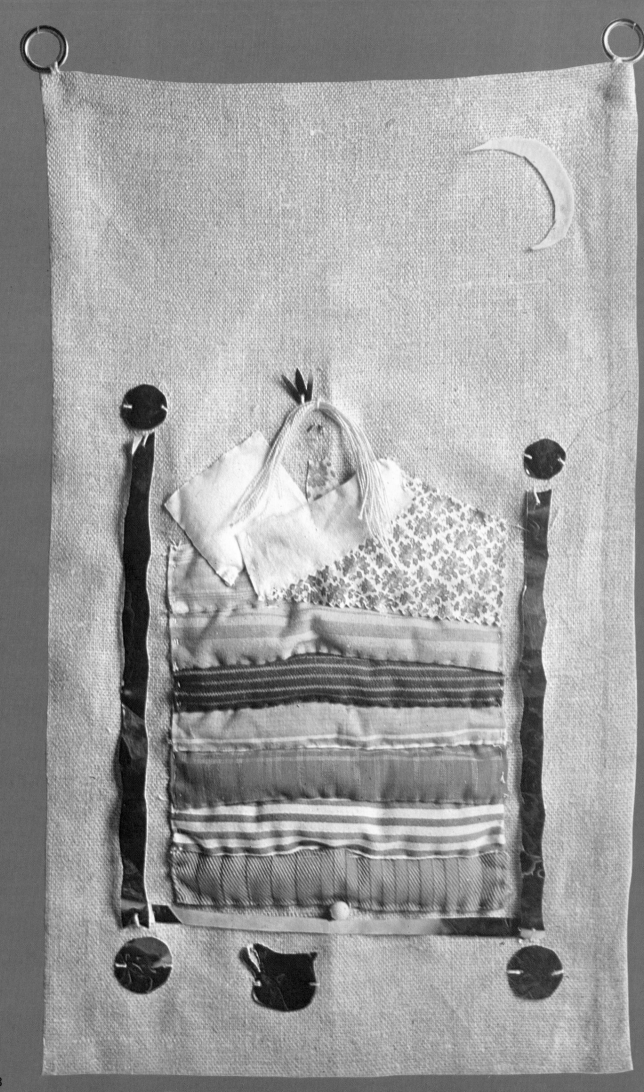

1688

# Stitchery design/fairy tale in embroidery

This delightful embroidery hanging illustrates the old fairy tale "The princess and the pea"—and there she is, uncomfortably feeling the pea through seven mattresses. It's simple to do and a young embroiderer might be encouraged to work it for her own bedroom wall.

The mattress pieces are stitched to the background on three sides, leaving the top open. Insert a small amount of teased-out absorbent cotton to pad the mattress and close the top with running stitches. Metal foil has been used for the bed frame, the chamber pot and the princess's crown. Cut out the shapes and then prick the stitching holes with a needle.

The foil shapes must be stitched very loosely to the background or the foil will be damaged by the stitches. The pea is a small white bead, stitched finally under the bottom mattress.

After hemming all four sides of the hanging, stitch two curtain rings to the upper corners.

The hanging illustrated was worked to a measurement of 13 inches deep by 8½ inches wide.

▼ *Two more fairy stories which would make companion wall panels,* Thumbelina *and the* Little Mermaid

# Stitchery pattern/floral pillow

This charming floral design pillow would look attractive in either a traditional or a modern decor.

To make this pillow measuring 15 inches square you will need:

☐ Pieces of single-weave canvas with 14 threads to 1 inch measuring 21 inches square
☐ Piece of fabric measuring 16 inches square for backing
☐ Zipper 10 inches long
☐ Tapestry needle No.18
☐ Pillow form measuring 16 inches square
☐ Appletons Crewel Yarn in the amounts indicated in the following column.

The entire design is worked using diagonal tent stitch, worked over two threads of canvas, with three strands of crewel yarn in the needle.

**To make the pillow**

When the stitchery is complete, block and trim the canvas leaving ½ inch seam allowances. Make into a pillow using a fabric backing. Leave a 10 inch opening on one side of the pillow and insert the zipper. Insert pillow form.

| | Color | No. | Skeins |
|---|---|---|---|
| 1 | Rose pink | 759 | 1 |
| 2 | Scarlet | 505 | 1 |
| 3 | Rose pink | 755 | 1 |
| 4 | Dull rose pink | 144 | 1 |
| 5 | Dull rose pink | 142 | 3 |
| 6 | Mauve | 607 | 3 |
| ○ | Mauve | 604 | 1 |
| ⋈ | Mauve | 602 | 1 |
| ⊡ | Putty | 981 | 2 |
| ⊟ | Putty | 983 | 2 |
| ⧄ | Putty | 985 | 1 |
| ◝ | Bright yellow | 553 | 1 |
| ⊡ | Lemon | 996 | 1 |
| ✎ | Chocolate | 187 | 1 |
| ▲ | Red brown | 208 | 1 |
| ⊠ | Honeysuckle yellow | 697 | 1 |
| ● | Drab green | 338 | 1 |
| ◥ | Drab green | 335 | 2 |
| △ | Drab green | 332 | 2 |
| ◉ | Drab green | 331 | 1 |
| ■ | Bright peacock green | 835 | 1 |
| ◺ | Bright peacock green | 832 | 1 |
| ⋉ | Bright peacock green | 831 | 1 |
| ⊘ | Peacock blue | 641 | 1 |
| ☐ | Background—off white | 992 | 12 |

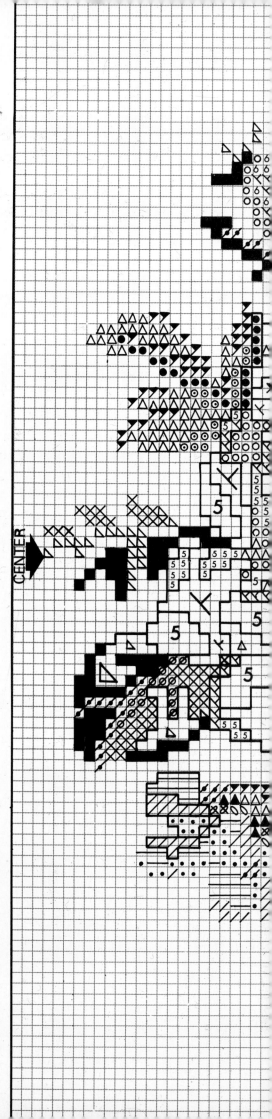

# Stitchery design/mola work

**San Blas appliqué**

Bold, brilliant colors are used in this unique method of appliqué, worked by the Indian women of the San Blas Islands off the coast of Panama. The appliqué designs are now worked in two pieces measuring about 14 inches by 20 inches and are made into blouses called molas.

When the Indians first moved to the islands in about 1850, the molas were simple affairs, made only of dark blue material with a single band of red cloth around the bottom. The designs developed to decorate the lower half of the mola and then developed further to form a major part of the blouse. Later, when traders brought fabrics of brighter colors to the islands, the designs became more elabor-

ate, involving up to five or six layers of fabric in as many colors. Reds, oranges, greens and blues vibrated together in one design. The designs themselves are primitive and gay, representing forms and figures from everyday life on the islands. Gods, goddesses, shapes from nature such as animals and plants and important people are all featured in bold, primitive stylized shapes. Often the designs are copied from pictures in magazines, comic books, calendars and even labels on canned foods. The designs often include English words or letters which are not understood by the Spanish speaking Indians and used with complete disregard of their meaning, but which look decorative and important. The stylized designs of the molas reflect

the style of the wooden figures called "nuchus", carved by the Sans Blas men. The layers of fabric are first basted together and then cut away, and the result very much resembles the enamel work of some Mexicans, where layers of color are applied (painted) then incised to reveal color on color.

The molas are an important status symbol amongst the Indians and in some places it is considered improper for a San Blas Indian girl to be married without possessing at least twelve or more unworn molas as part of her dowry.

**Fabrics**

For the traditional style San Blas appliqué, plain dyed fabrics such as poplin or

▲ *San Blas appliqué worked on the hem of a simple wrapover evening skirt*

sail cloth are ideal. However, pure silks or shantung would lend themselves beautifully to the technique. For the more ambitious, experiments with textured fabrics such as corduroy or tweed could prove interesting. Felt, suede or leather could also be used but no turnings would be needed.

## Uses

This appliqué technique is ideal for fashion where rich, bold effects are required. It would look good worked as a border on a skirt, on an evening cape, on inset panels or on a yoke on a dress or a blouse.

Mola work on curtains would look dramatic and pillow covers, bedspreads, pictures and wall hangings are all suitable subjects.

## Method

This appliqué technique is more a method of cutting away than applying pieces of fabric. Parts of the top layers of fabric are cut away to reveal a section of the color below. One, two or three layers of fabric may have to be cut through at the same time to get to the desired color for a particular part of the design. However, if the colors are arranged well, it should not be necessary to have to cut through more than one layer of fabric at a time. Pieces of different colors can be placed under only certain parts of the design.

Experiment with two or three layers of fabric to start with, introducing extra color by applying small areas of fabric to highlight the design.

Place the fabrics in the desired arrangement of colors then baste the layers of fabric together all around the edge and also diagonally across each way to hold them securely.

To reveal the first color under the top layer, use a pair of sharp embroidery scissors and cut away a portion of the top fabric in the desired shape. Clip the edges of the fabric to be turned under on all curves and into all corners and turn in $\frac{1}{8}$ inch. Using a matching color sewing thread, slip stitch the edge to the layer of fabric below. Small appliqués of another color can be added in one, two or more layers using the same technique of cutting out to reveal the color below.

# Home crochet/lacy lampshade

This extremely simple pattern for a lampshade cover can either be used to fit in with a room decor or to give new life to an old lampshade. Use the basic stitch pattern of straight and looped chain to make something else for your room to match up with the lampshade, such as a table mat, chair back cover or even curtains.

## Size

To fit drum lampshade 11in deep by 10in top diameter by 10½in bottom diameter.

**Gauge**
5 patts to 2¾ in worked on No.D hook.

## Materials

Coats & Clark's O.N.T. Speed-Cro-Sheen
5 100 yd balls
One No. C (2.50 mm) crochet hook
One No. D (3.00 mm) crochet hook
One purchased drum lampshade 11 in deep, 10 in top diameter, 10½ in bottom diameter

## Main section

Using No.D hook, ch192 loosely. Join with a ss into first ch.
**1st round** Ch7, 1sc into same ch as ss, ch2, skip 2ch, 1sc into next ch, *ch7, 1sc into same ch, ch2, skip 2ch, 1sc into next ch, rep from * to end, working last sc into a ss at beg of round. 64 patts.
**2nd round** Ss into center of first ch7 loop, *ch2, 1sc into next ch7 loop, rep from * to end, working last sc into center of first ch loop.
**3rd round** *Ch7, 1sc into same sc, ch2, 1sc into next sc, rep from * to end, working last sc into last sc of previous round.
The 2nd and 3rd rounds form patt and are rep throughout.
Continue in patt until work measures about 5½in.
Change to No.C hook and continue in patt until work measures 11in, ending with a 2nd round (1st patt round).

## Top picot edging

**Next round** *Ch4, 1sc into next sp, 1sc into next sc, rep from * to end. Fasten off.

## Lower picot edging

Using No.C hook, attach yarn to a ch into which sc have been worked.
Work 1sc, ch4 and 1sc into same ch, *1sc into each of the 2 skipped ch between groups of sc of first round, 1sc into next ch, ch4, 1sc into same ch, rep from * until 2ch remain, 1sc into each of next 2sc. Fasten off.

## Finishing

Press under a damp cloth, using a warm iron.
Place on lampshade and catch stitch in place around edges.

▼ *Several ideas for around the home to make from the basic stitch pattern*

*Cover to brighten a lampshade, new or old* ►

# Tailoring four

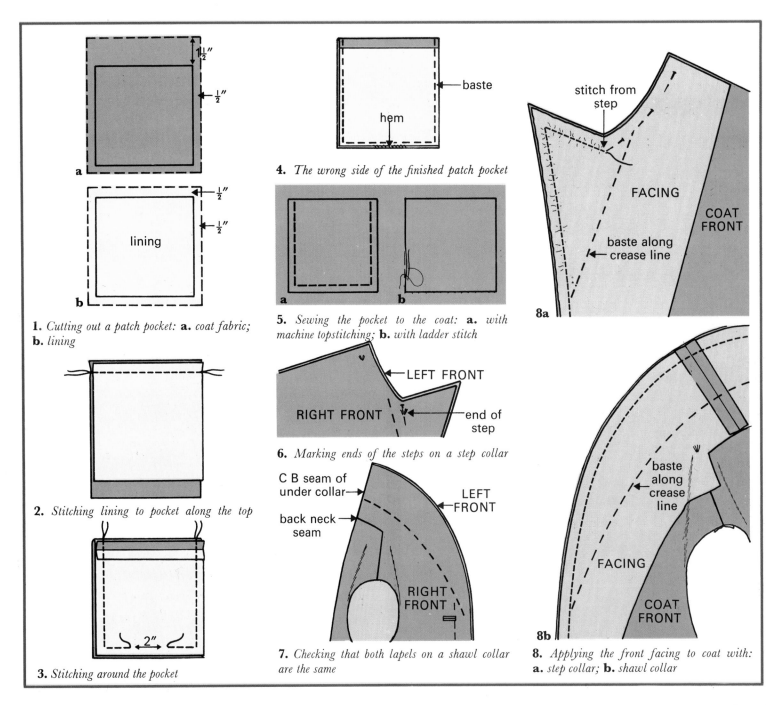

**1.** *Cutting out a patch pocket:* **a.** *coat fabric;* **b.** *lining*

**2.** *Stitching lining to pocket along the top*

**3.** *Stitching around the pocket*

**4.** *The wrong side of the finished patch pocket*

**5.** *Sewing the pocket to the coat:* **a.** *with machine topstitching;* **b.** *with ladder stitch*

**6.** *Marking ends of the steps on a step collar*

**7.** *Checking that both lapels on a shawl collar are the same*

**8.** *Applying the front facing to coat with:* **a.** *step collar;* **b.** *shawl collar*

---

**In this chapter**
**A. Patch pockets**
**B. Facing the coat front:** coat with lapels; coat without lapels.
**C. Belts:** belt across back; $\frac{1}{4}$ belt at side seams; $\frac{1}{2}$ belt at back; tie belt; belt with buckle.
**D. The second fitting:** preparing for the fitting; the fitting stages; set in sleeve; raglan sleeve.
**\*Terms and stitches**

## A. Patch pockets

**1a, b.** Cut out pocket shape with $\frac{1}{2}$ inch seam allowance all around plus an extra 1 inch along top edge (**a**). Then cut out lining 1 inch shorter than the pocket (**b**).
1696

**2.** Stitch lining to pocket along the top, taking $\frac{1}{2}$ inch seam. Press seam open.
**3.** Fold lining to pocket as shown, right sides facing. Stitch, leaving a 2 inch opening at the lower edge. Snip curved seams if any or snip across corners.
**4.** Turn through the opening, baste flat around edges and hem opening to close. Press and clap.
**5.** Apply to coat by topstitching (**a**) or ladder stitch\* (**b**).

## B. Facing the coat front

**Coat with lapels**
**6.** If working on a step collar mark the steps on the top edges of the lapels so they are both the same.

**7.** If working on a shawl collar, stitch and press the center back seam of the under collar, then stitch the shoulder and back neck seams. Press open and clap. Fold the coat in half and check that both sides have the same curve.
**8a, b.** Lay the facing and coat right sides together. Baste with small stitches to control the slight fullness there may be on the facing of the lapels.
Baste along crease line.
Stitch carefully as given on the instruction sheet, being careful to keep both lapels the same. Note that the step collar is only stitched as far as the end of the step.

*This coat from Vogue Patterns has welt pockets and a tie belt* ►

1697

**9a, b.** Remove basting. Snip across corners, snip into the end of the stitching line if applicable, and layer the seam allowances.

Press the seam open over a pressing roll.

**10a, b.** Turn facing to the inside. Working on the underside of the lapel, baste the seam edge of the lapel so that it lies away from the top edge and baste along the crease line. Baste the remainder of the facing seam to lie away from the top of the coat.

To press the lapel lay it flat, right side down, on an ironing board. Cover with a damp cloth and press as far as the crease line. Clap.

Press and clap the rest of the front edge. Lay the coat right side up with lapel folded in position and lightly press over a ham, using a woolen cloth under the pressing cloth.

Press the wrong side of the lower coat on a flat board.

**11.** Side stitch* under the lapel and down the inside front to keep the seam in position.

### Coat without lapels

Apply the facing as given on your pattern instruction sheet and follow the steps given above for coats with lapels, ignoring those points referring specifically to the lapels.

**12.** The whole of the front seam edge should be basted to lie toward the inside of the coat and then side stitched* as shown.

## C. Belts

You can add your own belt to a plain coat to give back interest.

**13a—e.** The belt can be set into the side seams and go right across the back (**a**). It can be set into the side seams and sewn or buttoned at the side back (**b**). It can be set across the center back (**c**). You can have a tie belt (**d**) or a buckled belt (**e**).

**14.** For all belts you will need two pieces of the coat fabric each to the required width plus ½ inch seam allowance all around and one piece of interfacing cut to the same measurements.

**15.** If you are making buttonholes, baste the interfacing to the wrong side of one belt piece and make the buttonhole, as shown.

**16.** Place the belt pieces together, right sides facing, and lay the interfacing on the top. Baste together.

### Belt across back

**17.** Stitch the long edges, layer the seam allowances, turn, baste and press.

**18.** Topstitch to match coat if required.

1698

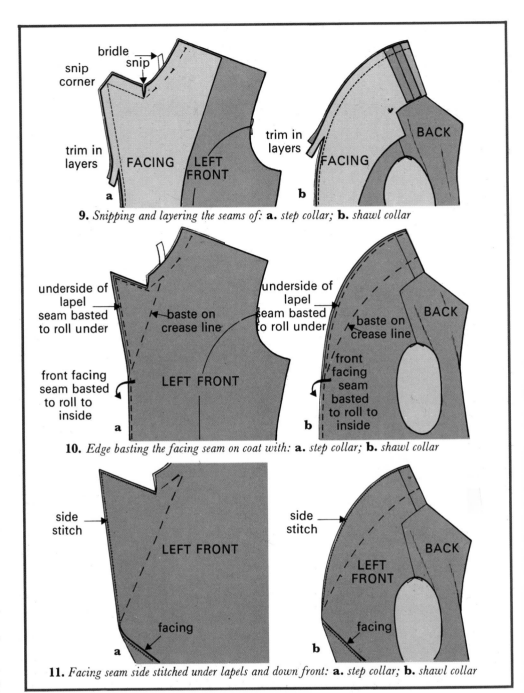

**9.** *Snipping and layering the seams of:* **a.** *step collar;* **b.** *shawl collar*

**10.** *Edge basting the facing seam on coat with:* **a.** *step collar;* **b.** *shawl collar*

**11.** *Facing seam side stitched under lapels and down front:* **a.** *step collar;* **b.** *shawl collar*

**19a, b.** When fitting make sure the belt is correctly balanced for the figure, usually above the waist for a short figure (**a**) and below the waist for a tall figure (**b**).

### Quarter belt at side seams

**20.** Make buttonholes and shape the end.

**21.** Stitch long edges and across shaped end.

Snip and layer the seam allowances, turn, baste and press.

Topstitch if required.

**22a, b.** When fitting make sure that both belts are balanced and the same length. The belt should be just above the waist for a short figure (**a**) and just below the waist for a tall figure (**b**).

### Half belt at back

**23.** Make buttonholes and shape ends.

**24.** Stitch the belt all around leaving a 2 to 4 inch opening along one side.

Snip and layer the seam allowances, turn, baste and press. Hem opening to close.

Topstitch if required.

When fitting check for balance as for the belt across the back (figure **19**).

### Tie belt

**25.** Make as for ½ belt at back.

### Belt with buckle

Make up as for ¼ belt.

**26.** Fold unstitched end through buckle. Turn under raw ends and herringbone.

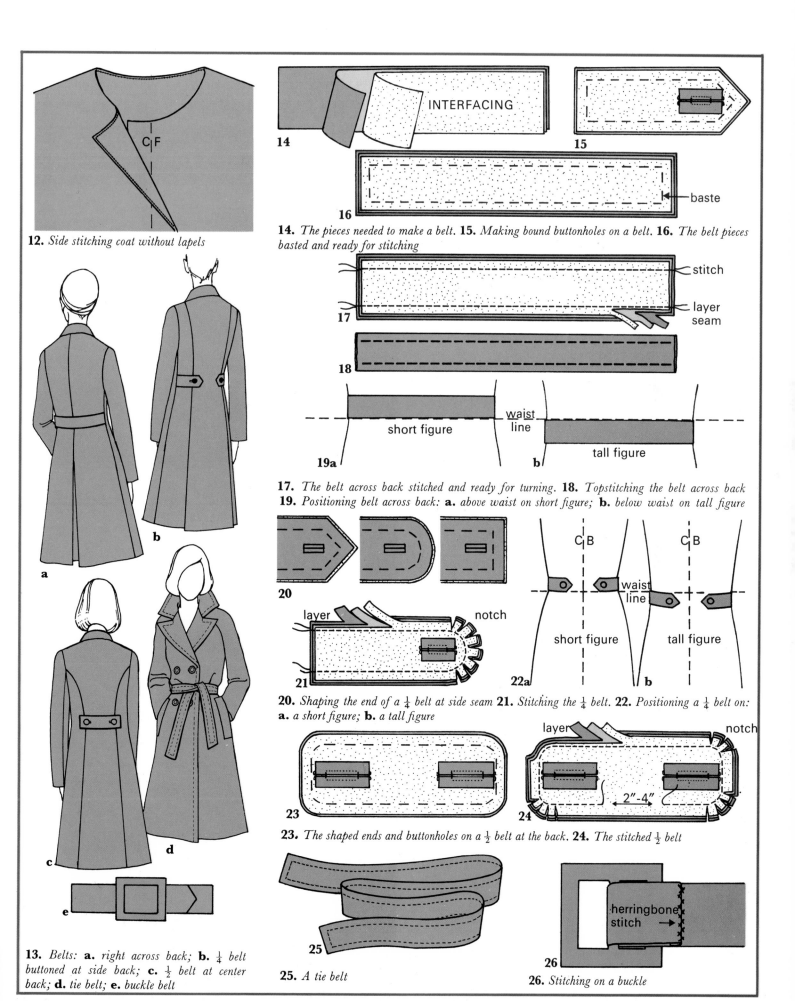

**12.** *Side stitching coat without lapels*

**13.** *Belts:* **a.** *right across back;* **b.** *¼ belt buttoned at side back;* **c.** *½ belt at center back;* **d.** *tie belt;* **e.** *buckle belt*

INTERFACING

baste

**14.** *The pieces needed to make a belt.* **15.** *Making bound buttonholes on a belt.* **16.** *The belt pieces basted and ready for stitching*

stitch

layer seam

short figure · waist line · tall figure

**17.** *The belt across back stitched and ready for turning.* **18.** *Topstitching the belt across back* **19.** *Positioning belt across back:* **a.** *above waist on short figure;* **b.** *below waist on tall figure*

layer · notch

C B · waist line · C B
short figure · tall figure

**20.** *Shaping the end of a ¼ belt at side seam* **21.** *Stitching the ¼ belt.* **22.** *Positioning a ¼ belt on:* **a.** *a short figure;* **b.** *a tall figure*

layer · notch · 2"-4"

**23.** *The shaped ends and buttonholes on a ½ belt at the back.* **24.** *The stitched ½ belt*

**25.** *A tie belt*

herringbone stitch

**26.** *Stitching on a buckle*

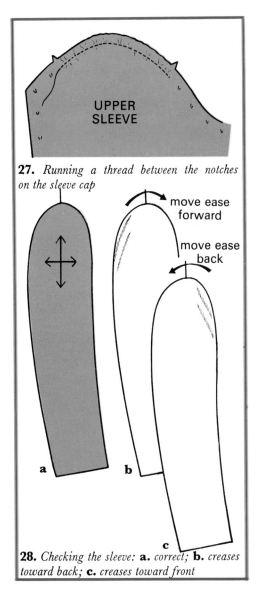

**27.** *Running a thread between the notches on the sleeve cap*

move ease forward

move ease back

**28.** *Checking the sleeve:* **a.** *correct;* **b.** *creases toward back;* **c.** *creases toward front*

▲ *Close-up of a raglan sleeve set in position. From Butterick pattern 6528*

## D. The second fitting

Having made the coat fronts, belt (if required) and stitched the back seams, it is now time for the second fitting.

### Preparing for the fitting
Working on the new fitting lines, baste the side seams. Baste the shoulder seams if not already sewn. Over baste the under collar (Tailoring 2, A, page 1656).
**27.** Sew a running thread between the notches on the sleeve caps to help distribute the ease and baste the sleeves into the armholes.
Add shoulder pads if required.

### The fitting stages
☐ Check all the points made in Tailoring 2, page 1656.
☐ Turn up the hem. If the coat has a tie or buckled belt, put on the belt before adjusting the hem as the length will be affected.
☐ Other belts are positioned after the

hem has been turned up. The coat must not be cut in half by a belt, it should give a balanced, pleasing look.
☐ Check the length again with the belt in position.
☐ Check that the sleeve is not too tight or too loose.
☐ Turn up the sleeve hem.

### Set in sleeve
**28a.** Take a good look at each sleeve cap. The grain should be square and there should be no creases.
**28b.** If there are creases toward the back, unbaste and move the ease slightly toward the front. If this is not enough then unbaste the complete sleeve and move it forward.
**28c.** If there are creases toward the front then reverse the process moving the ease to the back.

### Raglan sleeve
Check that the sleeves are not too full at the shoulders. Any fullness should be

pinned into the dart or seam which runs down the shoulder into the arm.

## *Terms and stitches

**Ladder stitch (29):** used for invisibly stitching a pocket to a garment.

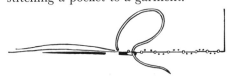

**Side stitch (30):** used for flattening edges of lapels and collars. Make a tiny stitch at right angles to the line of stitching. The stitches should not appear on the right side of the garment.

# Crafts/making lampshades

## Choosing shapes
Lighting plays an important part in home decoration, and a well-placed lamp with a tastefully designed shade can contribute a great deal to the restful atmosphere and charm of almost any room. When considering a shade, choose a style, size and color that will not be out of harmony with the lamp base.

## Colors and lamp bases
Some colors are generally thought to be more suitable for lampshades than others. Good colors include gold, pink, red and green, although any color is acceptable if it fits into the color scheme of the room and enhances the overall effect of the furnishings. Generally, blue and dead white shades tend to give a rather harder light than gold and red.

Bases for lamps require a lot of thought and it is advisable to take the base to the store when choosing the shade frame, to see that the size and shape balance the base. A wide variety of ready-made bases are available but it is often possible to pick up a lovely old vase in your local junk shop and convert it. Old brass and silver candlesticks also make elegant bases and it is often worth spending a few dollars to have them properly converted. Wine decanters and bottles rarely make good bases for lampshades.

## Cover material and lining
When selecting cover material for a soft lampshade, choose a fabric with plenty of "give", e.g. crepe back satin, rayon dupioni, wild silk and Thai silk. Heavy home furnishing fabrics, cottons, nylons, and materials that do not stretch are not suitable for fitted lampshades.

Crepe back satin is the best choice for lining as it has plenty of give, is reasonably priced, has a shiny surface to reflect light, and is very easy to work. Japanese silk is suitable for small shades only and it is

▲ *Instructions are given for making this empire lampshade*

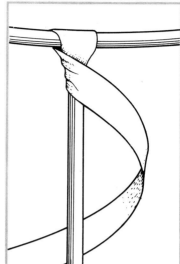

*Above left and right: first two stages in taping, figure* **1**

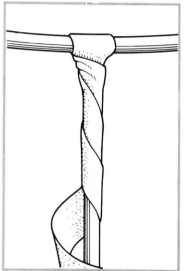
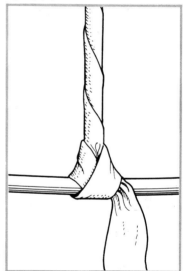

*Above left and right: winding and finishing off*

not as easy to use as crepe back satin.

The lining of a lampshade has two purposes; to hide the struts, particularly with pendant shades, and to give warmth to an otherwise cold light. A peach or pink lining, for instance, would give a warm glow to a white cover. Different effects can be achieved by using colored linings. A white lining reflects the light and is a good choice when the cover material is dark.

### Trimmings

Trimmings can make or mar a lampshade. Before deciding which trimming to use, first consider the type of lampshade being made and the room in which it is to be used. Tailored shades often look most effective with a plain trimming and are easily spoiled by a fussy one.

There are many attractive commercially-made trimmings from which to choose, in various widths and textures, but for a tailored effect try making the trimming

from a piece of bias strip cut from the cover material. A well made and well applied bias strip can look very elegant. It should be made with care and needs "practice to make perfect", but is well worth the extra effort involved. Metallic braids and laces look well used in conjunction with a bias strip trim.

### Frames and fitting

The frame and fitting is the first consideration and is the basis of a successfully made lampshade.

Choose a frame made from a good firm wire (copper if possible) and one free from rough edges. If necessary file down any rough edges or they may poke through the binding tape. Check also that the frame is not bent because this is difficult to remedy.

It is advisable to paint the frame with a good gloss paint (allowing a day or two to dry thoroughly) as this reduces the risk of the frame rusting when it is washed.

## Making an empire lampshade

To make a 10 inch bowed empire lampshade with a balloon lining you will need the following:

- ☐ Sharp pair of scissors
- ☐ Needles—sharps 9 for making silk shades
- ☐ Steel dressmaking pins or glass headed pins
- ☐ Good adhesive—UHU
- ☐ $\frac{3}{8}$in rayon seam tape
- ☐ Soft pencil
- ☐ Thimble
- ☐ Matching silk
- ☐ $\frac{1}{2}$yd 36 inch fabric for the cover
- ☐ $\frac{1}{2}$yd 36 inch fabric for the lining

### Binding the frame

This is a vital process in the making of a lampshade; if it is not done well, the cover and lining will be loose and baggy instead of taut and firm. For each strut allow twice its length in seam tape. For top

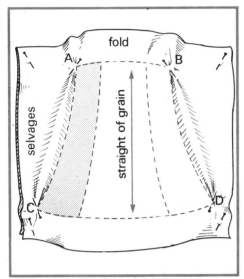

**▲ 2.** *Placing the first four pins, figure 2*

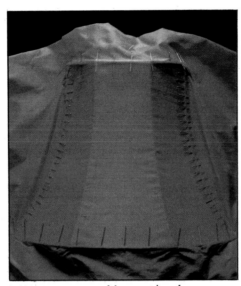

**▲** *Side struts, top and bottom pinned*

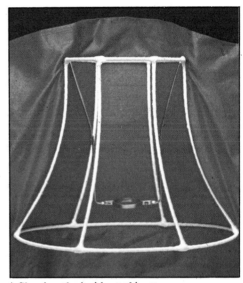

**▲** *Showing the inside at this stage*

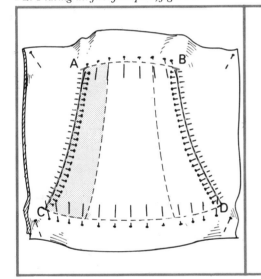

**▲ 3.** *Marking struts with a pencil line*

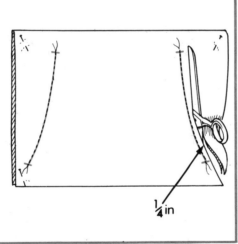

¼ in

**▲ 4.** *Cutting along machining line*

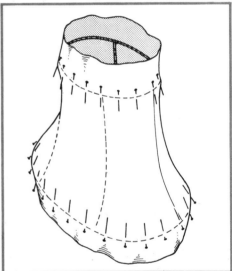

**▲ 5.** *Pinning top and bottom rings*

and bottom rings allow twice their circumference. If too much tape is used the struts become bulky and uneven.

Great care must be taken when taping the frame to make sure that the binding is both tight and smooth on the struts and rings. Tape each strut separately and then tape top and bottom rings. Always start and finish taping at the join of a strut and ring, otherwise the tape may work loose. Knot the tape exactly as illustrated. No sewing is necessary, except when braiding rings for hard lampshades where there are no struts (figure **1**).

**Fitting fabric onto frame**

Fold the cover fabric in half and, with right sides together, place one pin in each corner to hold the pieces together. Place material onto one side only of the frame with the fold at the top and the grain running from the top of the frame to the bottom.

Place a pin at A, B, C, and D to hold

the fabric to the frame (figure **2**).

Start pinning fabric to the side struts (AC and BD), placing pins every ½ inch. Do not pin on top and bottom rings yet, although some wrinkles will appear on the material. Check with the photograph illustrating this stage.

Make sure pins are placed on the side struts with the heads facing the center of the lampshade—this lessens the risk of damaging clothes and body. Now pin the top and bottom. Tighten the fabric as you go, just enough to remove the wrinkles, pinning every 1½ inches and facing pins inward. Complete pinning down the side struts by inserting pins every ¼ inch.

Mark down the struts over the pins with a soft pencil extending pencil line ½ inch beyond the last pin on AB and CD and making a pencil mark ½ inch around the top and bottom ring (figure **3**).

Take out the pins from the frame but keep the holding corner pins in position.

Stitch down the pencil line from top to bottom, using a medium-sized stitch; stretch fabric very slightly while doing this so that when it is pulled onto the frame the stitches do not break (figure **4**).

Trim the fabric away ¼ inch from the stitching line at each side. Cut along the fold at the top edge but do not cut anything at the bottom.

Prepare the lampshade lining in exactly the same way.

**Putting the cover on**

Press the cover flat (do not press seams open) and slip it over frame with right side outside, making sure that the seams are placed on the side struts. Match horizontal pencil line to top and bottom rings. Pin top and bottom of side seams and then tighten fabric and pin every 1 inch around top and bottom rings (figure **5**). Once again make sure that the pins are correctly placed to avoid unnecessary damage to clothes.

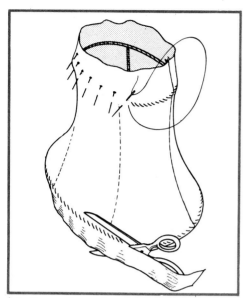

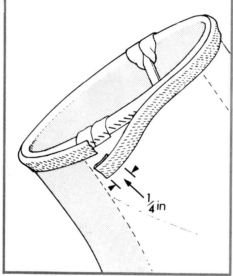

**▲8.** *Making gimble neat with bias strip*
**▼9.** *Applying bias strip trimming*

**▲6.** *Oversewing to frame and trimming*
**▼7.** *Pinning lining to the frame*

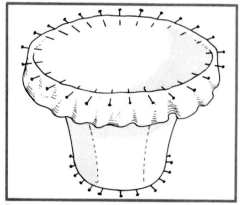

$\frac{1}{4}$ in

**▼** *Three more lampshades which can be made following the technique given for the empire shape*

Oversew the cover to the frame using a No.9 sharps needle and a short length of double matching silk thread. If too long a piece of thread is used it will catch around the pins; it is better to use several short lengths. The stitching should be on the outside edge of the top and bottom rings and the oversewing should be done from right to left. Trim away surplus material from top and bottom of lampshade, cutting right up to the stitches (figure **6**).

### Inserting balloon lining

Drop the prepared lining into the shade, matching seams and match horizontal pencil marks to top and bottom rings. Pin around top and bottom rings keeping pins on outside edge of lampshade (figure **7**). Tighten the lining by adjusting the pins at top and bottom rings until there is no fullness left. Stitch lining in the same way as the cover, making sure that the stitches come on the outside edge of the lampshade. These will then be completely covered by the trimming.

Note: when fitting the fabric around the top ring, rip the seam down to the horizontal pencil mark and splay out the material to enable the lining to fit neatly around the gimble. Do not try to join up material.

### Making gimble neat

Cut a piece of bias strip 1 inch wide and 4 inches long. Turn in $\frac{1}{4}$ inch at each side to make $\frac{1}{2}$ inch wide strip. Press. Slip under gimble (figure **8**). Pin in position and oversew in the same way as for the balloon lining, being careful to keep the stitches on the outside edge of the top ring.

### Bias trimming

Measure around top and bottom of lampshade and prepare enough bias to fit around top and bottom of shade plus 2 inches for turnings. Prepare this in the same way as for the gimble finishing (figure **12a**). Make sure the material is cut on the direct bias and that any joins necessary are made on the bias.

Starting at the side seam apply end of bias strip to outside edge of lampshade, beginning $\frac{1}{4}$ inch beyond seam.

Apply adhesive carefully and evenly to bias strip, spreading with a small knife. Great care is needed in applying the adhesive, because it will mark the fabric if it is used carelessly.

Stretch the bias strip slightly when applying it to the lampshade, pressing it gently with fingers to make it firm. The bias should just cover the oversewing stitches and should not extend to the inside of the shade. When the strip has been

*Two modern lampshades complement William Morris wallpapers, printed from the original pearwood blocks*

applied to the top of the lampshade cut off the excess, turn under ¼ inch at one end and glue it over the other end (figure **9**). Apply the trim to the bottom edge of the lampshade in the same way, making sure both joins are on the same side of the shade.

## Hard lampshades

Hard lampshades are quick and easy to make, and attractive shades can be achieved with a minimum of effort. There are many attractive ready-made materials available from good handicraft shops, but it is also possible to make your own. Use an adhesive parchment to which the material of your choice can be ironed, pressing the material onto the adhesive side with a hot iron. If this method is used, it is advisable to use materials that will withstand a hot iron. The most suitable needles for making hard shades are betweens 5/6. A number of wooden clothes pins are also required. The two lampshades illustrated on this page are hard lampshades. The one on the left requires a pattern; the other is the simplest of all shapes to make.

## To make a drum lampshade

Two rings are used for a straight-sided drum lampshade. They must be the same size, but one should be plain and the other should have a fitting, pendant or gimble. Prepare the rings and tape as for the soft lampshade, finishing off the tape on the rings with a few oversewing stitches to keep it firm. Measure around the taped rings for the circumference and decide on the height required for the lampshade.

Cut a pattern from stiff paper or cardboard to test on the rings. Allow ¼ inch at the end for the overlap at the seam.

Fit the paper pattern onto the rings with wooden clothes pins and test the height of the shade and the fit of the pattern. Adjust if necessary. Cut fabric using the paper pattern and attach to the rings with clothes pins. Sewing from left to right and using a blanket stitch sew around top and bottom rings. Sew through the lampshade material and onto the tape. This gives a firm finish and the stitches will be covered by the trimming.

When top and bottom rings have been sewn the seam should be glued down. Press down firmly with fingers and hold

until stuck.

With a good adhesive apply trimmings to top and bottom of shade, turning in ends ¼ inch and butting together. The joins of the trimming should be on the seam of the lampshade.

### Making a pattern

This is the quickest and easiest way to obtain a pattern for a lampshade which is smaller at the top than at the bottom: i.e. a cone shape or near drum with side struts. Take a large sheet of cardboard or stiff paper. Placing lampshade frame on paper, draw with a pencil down the side strut and mark top and bottom.

Rotate frame very slowly, marking along the top and bottom rings until the first mark is reached. Allow ½ inch for seam allowance at the end; this can be trimmed down to ¼ inch later. Cut out and try pattern onto frame, adjusting if necessary. Note: always try the pattern before cutting into the lampshade fabric.

Cut out fabric from pattern and proceed in the same way as for the straight-sided drum.

This method can be used for making small wall light lampshades.

# Crochet pattern/lacy patterned jacket

Crochet this pretty jacket in a lacy pattern.

## Sizes

Directions are for 34/36in bust.
The figures in brackets [ ] refer to the 37/39in bust size.
Length, 21[22½]in.
Sleeve seam, 17[17½]in.

### Gauge

One rep of patt (one gr and one "V") and 4 rows to 2in on No.E hook.

## Materials

Reynolds Parfait
17[19] 30 grm balls
One No. E (3.50 mm) crochet hook
4 buttons

## Back

Using No.E hook, ch80[88].
**1st row** 1sc into second ch from hook, *1sc into next ch, rep from * to end. 79[87]sc.
**2nd row** Ch1 to count as first sc, *1sc into next sc, rep from * to end.
Rep 2nd row twice more.
**5th row** Ch3, skip next 2sc, *5dc into next sc—called 1gr —, skip 3sc, 1dc, ch2, and 1dc into next sc—called 1 "V"—, skip 3sc, rep from * to last 4sc, 1gr into next sc, skip 2sc, 1dc into last sc. 9½[10½] patts.
**6th row** Ch3, *1 "V" in center dc of gr, 1gr in 2ch sp of "V", rep from * to last gr, 1 "V" in center dc of gr, 1dc into 3rd of 3ch.
**7th row** Ch3, *1gr in 2ch sp of "V", 1 "V" in center dc of gr, rep from * to last "V", 1gr in 2ch sp of "V", 1dc in 3rd of 3ch.
Rep 6th and 7th rows until work measures 13½[14½]in from beg, ending with a 7th row.

### Shape armholes

**Next row** Ss over gr, ch3, 1gr into 2ch sp of next "V", patt to last "V", 1gr into 2ch sp of "V", 1dc into first dc of gr. Turn.
Rep the last row twice more. 6½[7½] patts.
Continue without shaping until armholes measure 7½[8]in, ending with a 7th patt row.
1706

### Shape shoulders

**Next row** Ss over first gr and "V", patt to last "V". Turn.
**Next row** Ss over first "V" and gr, patt to last gr. Turn. Fasten off.

## Left front

Using No.E hook, ch40[48].
Work as given for Back until work measures the same as Back to armholes, ending with a 7th patt row. 4½[5½] patts.

### Shape armhole and front edge

**Next row** Ss over first gr, ch3, patt to end.
Continue dec at armhole edge on next 2 rows as for Back, *at the same time* dec one st at front edge of next 4[8] rows, then every other row until 1[1½] patts have been dec at front edge. 2[2½] patts.
Continue without shaping until armhole measures the same as on Back, ending at armhole edge.

### Shape shoulder

**Next row** Ss over first gr and "V", patt to end. Fasten off.

## Right front

Work to correspond to left Front, reversing all shapings.

## Sleeves

Using No.E hook, ch40.
Work first 7 rows as given for Back. 4½ patts.
Continue in patt, inc one st at each end of next and every following 3rd row until one whole patt has been inc at each side. 6½ patts.
Continue without shaping until sleeve seam measures 17[18½]in, ending with a 7th patt row.
**NB.** On the second size the last inch is set into armhole shaping and is not included in sleeve seam measurement.

### Shape cap

**First size only. Next row** Ss over first gr, ch3, patt to last gr, 1dc into first dc of gr. Turn.
**Both sizes.** Dec 2 sts at each

end of every row until 1½ patts rem. Fasten off.

## Bands

### Left front

Using No.E hook, ch10.
**1st row** 1sc into 2nd ch from hook, *1sc into next ch, rep from * to end. 9sc.
Continue in sc until band, when slightly stretched, is the same length as Front edge to beg of shaping, ending with a WS row.
Inc one st at beg of next row, then at this same edge on every 5th row until 17 inc have been made.
Continue without shaping until band is same length as front edge to shoulder measured with band slightly stretched, ending with a WS row.
Fasten off.
Baste band in place and mark position of buttons with pins as follows. Place first pin about 2in from beg, 2nd pin about ¾in below beg of front shaping, then two more pins at equal distances between these two.

### Right front

Work to correspond to left front, reversing shaping and working buttonholes to correspond with pin positions.
**Buttonhole row** (RS) Ch1, 2sc, ch4, skip 4sc, 2sc.
**Next row** Ch1, 1sc, 4sc in ch4 loop, 3sc.

## Collar

Join shoulder seams.
With RS facing, work in sc across 17sc of right front Band, across Back neck, then across 17 sts of left front Band.
Continue in sc for 2in.
Fasten off.

## Finishing

Press lightly.
Sew in sleeves. On 2nd size sew the last inch of sleeve seams to first bound-off group at armholes.
Join side sleeve seams. Sew on front bands. Sew on buttons.

*Crocheted jacket for cooler days* ▶

1707

# Knitting pattern/jacket and skirt

This simple knitted suit has a slightly flared skirt which can be made to the length desired, and a jacket with frog fastenings and an interesting detail of slits at the sleeve edges.

### Sizes
Directions are for 34in bust. The figures in brackets [] refer to the 36, 38 and 40in sizes respectively.
**Jacket.** Length, 23½[24:24½:25]in.
Sleeve seam, 16[16½:17:17½]in.
**Skirt.** Length 20[21:22:23]in, adjustable.

> **Gauge**
> 6 sts and 8 rows to 1in over st st worked on No.5 needles.

### Materials
Reynolds Classique 50 grm balls
**Jacket.** 7[7:8:9] balls
**Skirt.** 4[5:6:6] balls
One pair No. 5 needles (or Canadian No. 8)
One No. E (3.50 mm) crochet hook
6 buttons
One 7 in zipper
Waist length elastic

## Jacket back

Cast on 108[114:120:126] sts.
K 15 rows.
**Next row** K12[12:11:11], *K up 1, K12[13:14:15], rep from * 6 times more, K up 1, K12[11:11:10]. 116[122:128:134] sts.
Beg with a K row, continue in st st for 3in, ending with a P row.
K2 tog at each end of next and every following 12th row until 108[114:120:126] sts rem.
Continue without shaping until work measures 16in from beg, ending with a P row.

### Shape armholes
Bind off 5[6:7:8] sts at beg of next 2 rows.
Bind off 2 sts at beg of next 2 rows.
K2 tog at each end of every other row 4 times.
86[90:94:98] sts.
Continue without shaping until armhole measures
1708

7½[8:8½:9]in, ending with a P row.

### Shape shoulders
Bind off 7[8:9:10] sts at beg of next 2 rows, then 9 sts at beg of following 4 rows.
Slip rem 36[38:40:42] sts on holder.

## Left front

Cast on 56[59:62:65] sts.
K 15 rows.
**Next row** K12, *K up 1, K12[13:14:15], rep from * twice more, K up 1, K8. 60[63:66:69] sts.
**Next row** K.
**Next row** K9, P to end.
Rep these 2 rows for 3in, ending with a WS row.
K2 tog at beg of next and every following 12th row until 56[59:62:65] sts rem, then continue without shaping until work measures the same as Back to armholes, ending with a WS row.

### Shape armhole
At arm edge, bind off 5[6:7:8] sts, then 2 sts once.
K2 tog at beg of every other row 4 times, at arm edge.
Continue without shaping on rem 45[47:49:51] sts until armhole measures 5¼[5½:5¾:6]in.
End with a WS row.

### Shape neck
**Next row** K34[35:36:37], turn and slip rem 11[12:13:14] sts on holder.
At neck edge, bind off 2 sts every other row twice.
Dec one st at neck edge on every other row until 25[26:27:28] sts rem.
Continue without shaping until armhole measures the same as on Back, ending with a P row.

### Shape shoulder
At arm edge, bind off 7[8:9:10] sts, then 9 sts once.
P 1 row.
Bind off rem 9 sts.

## Right front

Work to correspond to left Front, reversing all shaping.

## Sleeves

Cast on 26[28:30:32] sts.
K 15 rows.
**Next row** K5[6:7:8], (K up 1, K8) twice, K up 1, K5[6:7:8]. 29[31:33:35] sts*.
**Next row** K to end.
**Next row** P to last 5 sts, K5.
Rep last 2 rows until work measures 2½in, ending with a WS row. Break off yarn and place this piece on a spare needle.
Work a second piece in the same manner as far as *.
**Next row** K.
**Next row** K5, P to end.
Rep last 2 rows until work measures 2½in, ending with a WS row.
**Next row** K to end, then K across the sts of first piece on spare needle. 58[62:66:70] sts.
**Next row** P24[26:28:30], K10, P to end.
**Next row** K to end.
**Next row** P25[27:29:31], K8, P to end.
**Next row** K.
**Next row** P26[28:30:32], K6, P to end.
Continue to work 2 sts less in garter st in center of every other row until all sts are in st st.
Continue in st st, inc one st at each end of every 14th row until there are 72[76:80:84] sts.
Continue without shaping until sleeve seam measures 16[16½:17:17½]in. End with P row.

### Shape cap
Bind off 5 sts at beg of next 2 rows.
K2 tog at each end of every other row 13[14:15:16] times.
Bind off 2 sts at beg of next 10[10:12:12] rows, then 3 sts at beg of next 2 rows.
Bind off rem 10[12:10:12] sts.

## Neckband

Join shoulder seams.
With RS facing, K sts of right Front neck, pick up and K16 sts up side of neck, K Back neck sts, pick up and K16 sts down other side of neck, then K sts of left Front neck. 90[94:98:102] sts.

K 10 rows. Bind off.

### Frog fastenings
Using No.E hook, ch25.
Join into ring with a ss.
Into the ring work 14sc, ss into first sc (this makes buttonhole part) then continue around ring working 3sc, ch4, 1sc into the first of these 4ch, 12sc, ch4, 1sc into first of these 4ch, 3sc, ending with a ss into first sc.
Fasten off.
Make 5 more pieces in the same manner. Join into 3 pairs by stitching the ends of the longer loops together at the center of the 12sc.

## Skirt Back and Front alike

Cast on 88[92:96:100] sts.
K 16 rows.
Beg with a K row, work 4 rows st st.
**Next row** K22[23:24:25], K up 1, K2, K up 1, K40 [42:44:46], K up 1, K2, K up 1, K to end.
Work 7 rows.
**Next row** K23[24:25:26], K up 1, K2, K up 1, K42 [44:46:48], K up 1, K2, K up 1, K to end.
Continue inc in this manner on every 8th row 3[4:5:6] times more, then on every 16th row until there are 128[132:136:140] sts.
Continue without shaping until work measures 18[19:20:21]in, ending with a P row or to length desired.
**Next row** K8[10:7:9], *K2 tog, K8[8:9:9] rep from * 10 times more, K2 tog, K8[10:6:8]. 116[120:124:128] sts.
K 14 rows.
Bind off.

## Finishing

Press work lightly under damp cloth, using a cool iron.
**Jacket.** Sew in sleeves. Join side and sleeve seams. Press seams. Sew on buttons.
**Skirt.** Join seams leaving one side open at top for zipper. Sew in zipper. Sew elastic to waistband with casing-stitch. Press all seams.

1709

# Stitchery design / lattice smocking

Lattice smocking is worked without a foundation of gathering and produces an effective form of pleating on the right side of the fabric.

## Fabrics
Fabrics with a pile, such as velvet and corduroy, are the best to use, but any heavy quality fabric which does not crease easily, such as satin, will do. Allow approximately double the quantity of fabric to the required finished measurement.

## Threads
Use strong sewing threads such as buttonhole twist, button cotton or synthetic sewing thread in the needle.

## Method
Commercial transfers are made for stamping the dots used in the smocking, but it is possible to mark your own if you prefer. The dots are spaced in rows $1\frac{1}{4}$ inches apart.

All the smocking is worked on the wrong side of the fabric. The stitches will not show on the right side after the smocking pleats are formed. After the dots are marked on the wrong side of the fabric, start the smocking at the upper left-hand corner. Knot the end of the thread.

Pick up the dots by inserting the needle into the fabric to right of dot and out through the left side of the same dot. The thread is carried from dot to dot on the working side of the fabric. Pick up dot 1 with the needle and make a second holding stitch as shown in figure **1**. Then pick up dot 2, go back to dot 1 and pick up again as shown in figure **2**. Pull dots 1 and 2 together and knot securely as shown figure **3**. Pick up dot 3 then, with the thread above the needle, slip the needle under the thread between dots 1 and 2 as shown in figure **4**, pulling the thread tightly at dot 3 to form a knot. Be sure to keep the fabric flat between dots 1 and 3. Pick up dot 4, then go back and pick up dot 3 again as shown in figure **5**. Pull the dots together and knot them securely. Pick up dot 5 as shown in figure **6**, slip the needle under the thread between dots 3 and 5 and knot as in figure **4**. Continue to work down the row of dots in the same manner, starting with figure **2** and picking up dot 6 next. Secure all the ends firmly.

A different pattern may be obtained by leaving a 1 inch space between each worked row of smocking stitches, resulting in a chevron effect.

## Uses
This type of smocking is suitable as a decoration for pillows, hats, handbags, curtains, or items of dress.

*Far right: lattice smocking worked in velvet for the sleeves of this delightful dress*▶
▼ *Tracing guide to repeat as necessary*    *Step-by-step working instructions*▶

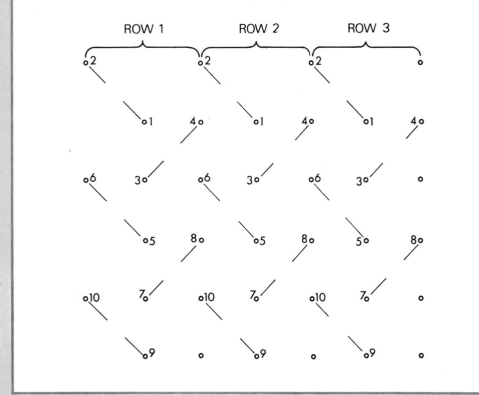

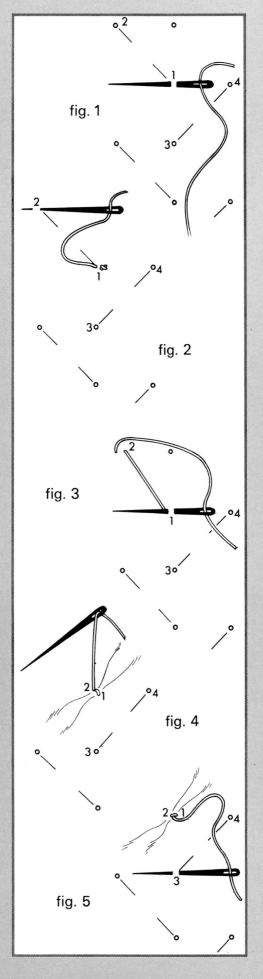

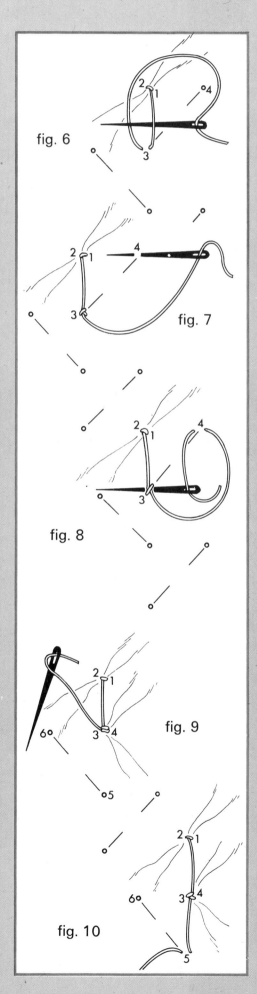

fig. 6

fig. 7

fig. 8

fig. 9

fig. 10

1712

# Stitchery pattern/blue town

This blue town picture is worked in a range of blue green shades with highlights of pink and white.

To make the picture, you will need:

☐ A piece of dark green linen measuring 23 inches by 16 inches
☐ A piece of hardboard measuring 18 inches by 11½ inches
☐ Crewel needle No. 8
☐ D.M.C. 6-strand floss in the following colors and amounts:

1. pale blue—747; 2. light blue—519; 3. medium blue—793; 4. dark medium blue—799; 5. blue—813; 6. light navy—792; 7. turquoise—807; 8. pale yellow—834; 9. lime—472; 10. light yellow—445; 11. gold—732; 12. dark green—987; 13. very dark green—986; 14. dark blue green—924; 15. medium gray green—502; 16. Pale gray green—503; 17. yellow green—471; 18. mauve—3041; 19. deep mauve—327; 20. dark slate blue—931; 21. pale pink—818; 22. deep pink—899; 23. white; 24. brown—838.

One skein each of colors:
6, 8, 9, 11, 12, 13, 16, 17, 18, 20, 21, 22, 23, 24
Two skeins each of colors:
1, 2, 3, 4, 5, 7, 10, 14, 15, 19

## Stitches

The stitches used to embroider this picture are running stitch, French knots and couching in a variety of simple methods. The flowers and leaves are worked in freely worked satin stitch.

Use four strands in the needle for the French knots and laid threads, and two strands for the couching and all other stitches. If preferred, small beads could be substituted for the French knots.

## Working

It is essential to work this picture in a square embroidery frame to keep the stitching flat and even.

## Finishing

When the embroidery is completed, lay over a thick, soft pad and press carefully to avoid flattening the French knots. Mount the picture over the hardboard.

# Home crochet/wallhanging

▲ *The wall hanging can be hung by either tacking directly to the wall or by mounting over a frame and then hanging as an ordinary picture*

Working in fabric strips can be swift and exciting. The simple patterns are based on circular or straight crochet, using traditional stitches in rounds or rows. The water lily hanging illustrated takes this a stage further, using the lines of the rows to create additional visual texture, and has the same impact as a brilliant modern painting. It
1714

is worked in separate sections which are then sewn together. This pattern could be used to make an attractive throw rug.

**Working in fabric strips**
Either of two sizes of crochet hook equally suitable for rag rugs, No. K (7.00 mm) and No. Jumbo ¾ in. The choice depends on final effect desired.

The larger hook will obviously create larger stitches and the work will grow quickly. The finer hook will naturally produce smaller stitches and it will take longer to work the same area. The work will also look finer. Use strips of not more than half an inch wide, the longer the better. Always join pieces in the center of a row by laying the two ends on

top of the previous row and working over them with the new piece. Start using a new strip on the last stage of a stitch (see Crochet Know-how 5, page 86, and 32, page 622).

## Water lily hanging

**Size**
This will depend on the width and thickness of the strips, and also on the hook size used.

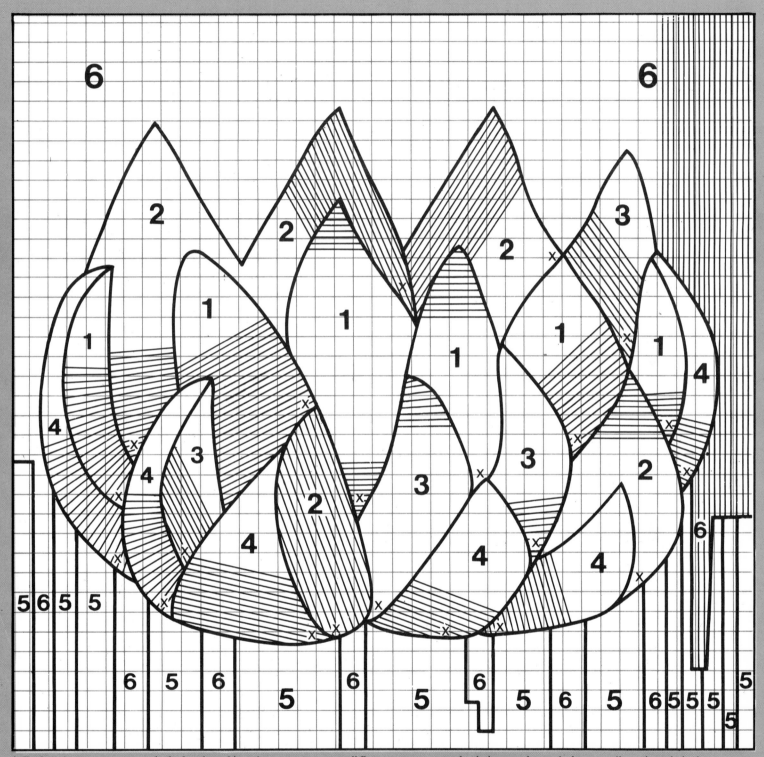

▲ *Each square represents one inch, but by taking them to represent a different measurement the design can be worked to any dimensions desired*

## Materials

This also depends on the hook size used and the finished size desired, but the following is a rough guide:
One No. Jumbo ¾in crochet hook
3yds cream, 1
4yds pale beige, 2
4yds medium beige, 3
3yds dark beige, 4
5yds blue green, 5
7 yds yellow green, 6

## Sections

Make actual size paper pattern pieces from the chart. Use single crochet throughout, working into the back loop of the stitch from right side of work and front loop from wrong side. Begin at the point marked X of each section. Work each area separately, continually measuring against the paper shape and increasing and decreasing as needed to produce the finished shape. Check with the chart and the illustration in which direction the stitches lie. If a section curves work part of the row, turn and work back, then work the next row across all stitches.

## Finishing

Sew the sections together on WS with matching sewing thread. Roll the hanging in a damp towel and leave for two hours. Pin out flat, WS up, and press with a warm iron to obtain a flat surface. Dry thoroughly.

# Tailoring five

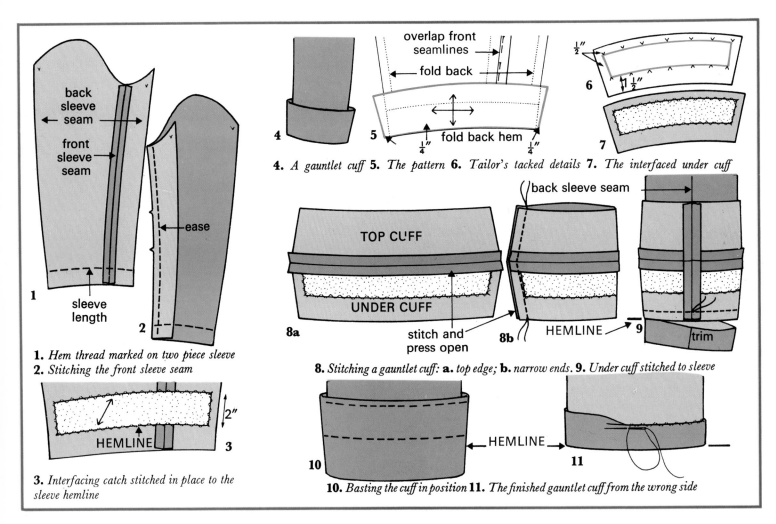

**1.** Hem thread marked on two piece sleeve
**2.** Stitching the front sleeve seam

**3.** Interfacing catch stitched in place to the sleeve hemline

**4.** A gauntlet cuff **5.** The pattern **6.** Tailor's tacked details **7.** The interfaced under cuff

**8.** Stitching a gauntlet cuff: **a.** top edge; **b.** narrow ends. **9.** Under cuff stitched to sleeve

**10.** Basting the cuff in position **11.** The finished gauntlet cuff from the wrong side

---

## In this chapter

**A. Plain tailored sleeve:** stitching the sleeve; finishing the hem edge.

**B. Gauntlet cuff:** cutting the pattern; making the cuff.

**C. Strap cuff:** cutting the pattern; making the cuff.

**D. Imitation vent opening on sleeve:** the pattern; making the sleeve.

**E. Two piece sleeve with vent opening.**

**F. Lining a sleeve:** plain sleeve lining; sleeve with a vent.

**\*Terms and stitches.**

## A. Plain tailored sleeve

Coat sleeves must be well fitted and have a crisp finish at the hem. With a two-piece tailored sleeve there is usually ease at the elbow level and great care must be taken while basting and stitching to keep this in the correct place and so prevent the sleeve from twisting.

### Stitching the sleeve

**1.** After fitting the sleeves rip the arm-hole basting. Thread mark the length. Mark any seam alterations. On a one-piece sleeve unbaste the sleeve seam. On a two-piece sleeve unbaste the back sleeve

seam only.

**2.** On a two-piece sleeve stitch the front sleeve seam and press open. If the sleeve has ease in it stitch carefully and press as for an eased seam.

### Finishing the hem edge

Cut a strip of interfacing in the bias grain of the fabric to the width of the sleeve and two inches deep.

**3.** Baste to the wrong side of the sleeve just above the hemline and catch stitch. Turn up the hem and press. Catch stitch to the interfacing.

## B. Gauntlet cuff

**4.** For a gauntlet cuff it is not necessary to interface the sleeve hem as it would be too bulky.

### Cutting the pattern

**5.** Place the two pieces of sleeve pattern together with the lower part of the front seamlines coinciding, and the hem and back seam allowances turned back. Cut the cuff pattern extending it $\frac{1}{4}$ inch each side at the hem edge and extending the top edge as style dictates. The cuff can be anything from 2 to 4 inches deep.

### Making the cuff

**6.** Using this pattern cut two pieces of coat fabric for each cuff adding $\frac{1}{2}$ inch seam allowance on the sides and top edge and $1\frac{1}{2}$ inches at the hem edge. Tailor's tack all around pattern.

**7.** Cut interfacing exactly to pattern, without seam allowance, and catch stitch to the under cuff section as shown.

**8a, b.** Stitch the cuffs together along the top edge (**a**). Then fold and stitch narrow ends together as shown (**b**).

**9.** Place the right side of the faced under cuff section to the right side of the sleeve. The cuff stitching line should be $\frac{1}{2}$ inch above the sleeve hemline and the cuff seam corresponding to the back sleeve seam as shown.

Stitch, trim seam allowance to $\frac{1}{2}$ inch.

**10.** Fold the top cuff over and baste along the top through both cuff layers only. Baste at hem through all fabric layers.

**11.** Turn the sleeve to the wrong side and catch stitch the lower edge of the

*Right: Vogue pattern, in green doeskin cloth, has a two-piece sleeve (because this fabric has a pile the coat was cut on the straight grain of the fabric). Far right: This Vogue pattern made in a home furnishing tapestry, has a cuffed sleeve.*

1717

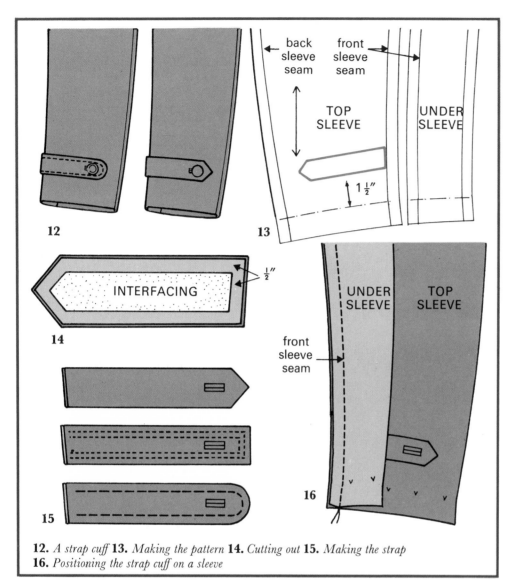

**12.** *A strap cuff* **13.** *Making the pattern* **14.** *Cutting out* **15.** *Making the strap*
**16.** *Positioning the strap cuff on a sleeve*

**17.** *Imitation vent opening*

**19.** *The interfaced hem edge*

**21.** *Pressed seam allowance on back seam*

---

cuff as shown, turning under the raw edge to make neat.

## C. Strap cuff

**12.** A strap cuff usually lies from the front seam of a two piece sleeve to the back seam, across the top of the sleeve.

### Cutting the pattern

**13.** Make a pattern for the strap, using the top sleeve pattern piece to give the correct angle. These straps usually end 1 inch from the back sleeve seam.
**14.** Cut the cuff from double fabric allowing $\frac{1}{2}$ inch all around for seams.
For each strap cut one piece of interfacing to pattern without seam allowance.

### Making the cuff

**15.** Make the cuff as for the $\frac{1}{4}$ belt in Tailoring 4, page 1696.
**16.** Baste to the front sleeve seam before the seam is sewn up.
Finish as for a plain sleeve.
1718

## D. Imitation vent opening on sleeve

**17.** Decide whether you would like this sleeve finish before you cut out the coat as additions have to be made to the back sleeve seam.

### The pattern

**18.** Cut an extension to each side of the back sleeve seam as shown. The extension should be $1\frac{1}{4}$ inches wide by the depth of the vent plus $\frac{3}{8}$ inch top and bottom for seam allowance.

### Making the sleeve

**19.** Stitch the front sleeve seam and baste interfacing to hem as shown. Make buttonholes on upper sleeve if required.
**20.** Baste and stitch the back sleeve seam as shown.
**21.** Snip the seam allowance on the under sleeve to allow the vent to lie on top of the sleeve. Then press the sleeve seam open above and below the vent.

Press the lower vent seam up.
**22.** Press hem up to vent opening and catch stitch to interfacing.

## E. Two piece sleeve with vent opening

**23.** Cut a strip of interfacing on the bias, wide enough to reach the top of the opening by the sleeve width, without seam allowance.
Make piped buttonholes to match the coat if required.
**24a, b, c, d.** The next step is to miter the corners. Cut away the corners $\frac{1}{8}$ inch from the interfacing (**a**). Fold up the $\frac{1}{8}$ inch and press (**b**). Turn hem up and sides in, snipping at top of opening (**c**). Catch stitch to canvas and draw stitch * mitered ends together (**d**).
**25.** Stitch the back sleeve seam.
Snip $\frac{1}{4}$ inch above vent then press seam open above snip and together below snip.
**26.** Baste vent in closed position and make a bar tack * at the top of the opening.

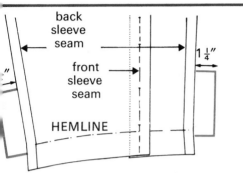

**18.** *Cutting extension on back sleeve seam*

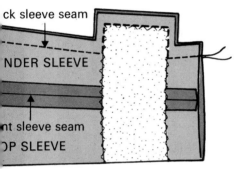

**20.** *Stitching the back sleeve seam*

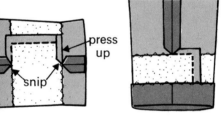

**22.** *The hem catch stitched in place*

**23.** *Vent opening with interfacing at hem edge*

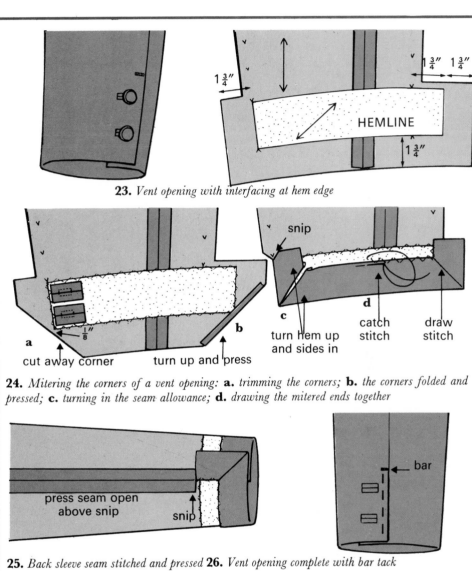

**24.** *Mitering the corners of a vent opening:* **a.** *trimming the corners;* **b.** *the corners folded and pressed;* **c.** *turning in the seam allowance;* **d.** *drawing the mitered ends together*

**25.** *Back sleeve seam stitched and pressed* **26.** *Vent opening complete with bar tack*

*Sleeve detail of plain cuff, Butterick pattern*

*Sleeve detail of vent opening, Butterick pattern*

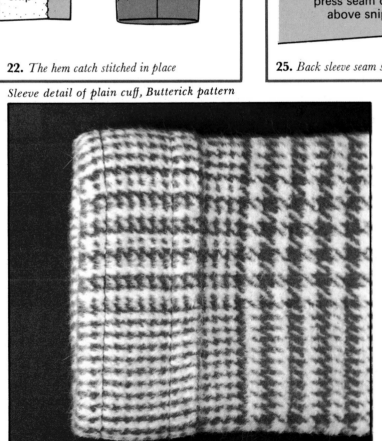

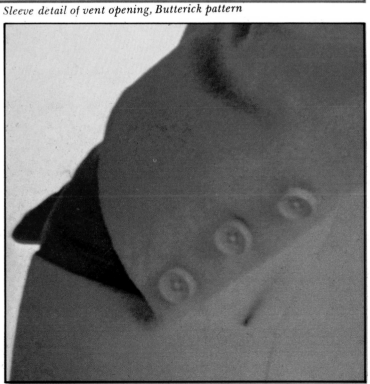

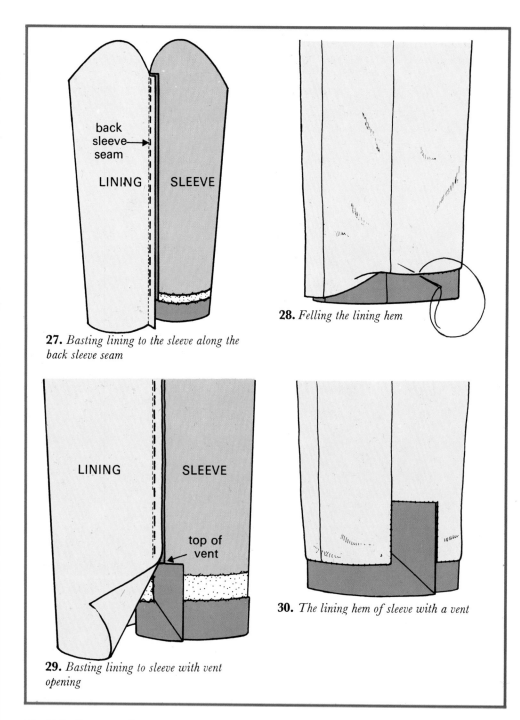

**27.** *Basting lining to the sleeve along the back sleeve seam*

**28.** *Felling the lining hem*

**29.** *Basting lining to sleeve with vent opening*

**30.** *The lining hem of sleeve with a vent*

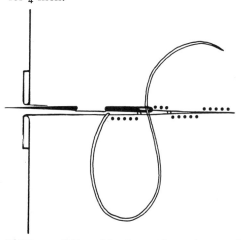

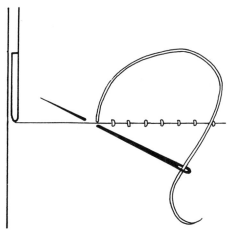

# *Terms and stitches

**Bar tack (31):** used to strengthen the top of a pleat or opening, and can be decorative as well as functional.

Using matching thread make a bar of 4 long stitches. Oversew tightly along the length of the stitches.

**Draw stitch (32):** used to close two folds of material together. Slip the needle through the top fold for $\frac{1}{4}$ inch. Then, directly under the end of the first stitch, slip the needle through the lower fold for $\frac{1}{4}$ inch.

**Felling (33):** this is a firm form of hemming with a stitch at right angles to the hem or fold.

# F. Lining a sleeve

The sleeve lining is sewn in place before the sleeve is stitched to the coat. It is much easier to do this now without the whole weight of the coat to contend with.

## Plain sleeve lining

The method used here is also applied to a sleeve with an imitation vent, cuff or strap finish.

Make the sleeve lining and press the seams open.

**27.** With wrong sides out, place the sleeve and lining side by side with back sleeve seams corresponding. Baste together along the seamline.

Turn the lining right side out over the sleeve.

**28.** Turn in the hem allowance of the lining and fell* to the sleeve.

## Sleeve with a vent

Make the sleeve lining, leaving the appropriate seam open below the vent.

**29.** With wrong sides out, place the sleeve and lining side by side, with the back sleeve seams corresponding. Baste seams together above the vent.

Turn the lining right side out over the sleeve.

**30.** Turn the raw lining edges under as shown and baste. Fell* lining to the sleeve.

# Crafts/suede and leathercraft

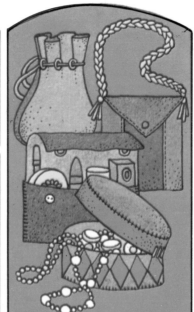

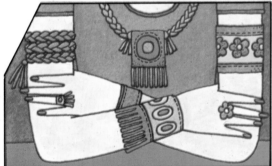

## New approach to leathercraft

One of the oldest of crafts, leather work fell into obscurity at the end of the nineteen-thirties, when pride in craftsmanship gave way to mass production. Thonging, as a means of joining two pieces of leather, was out, and fashion demanded that craftsmanship did not show, and that the article bore as close a resemblance to the machine-made as was possible.

A gayer, livelier interpretation of the original craft has now developed, losing none of the old standards yet making use of modern techniques. The essence of current fashion is reflected in the choice of materials and colors, and the way in which designers are now using suede and leather shows an exciting awareness of the scope of natural fibers.

To be able to design and make exciting and luxurious looking garments and accessories in leather and suede, it is important to know a little about the different kinds of leather and the best uses for them.

## Different kinds of leather

For most of the items a beginner will want to attempt, sheepskin is probably the best skin to use. It is supple, easily obtainable and falls into the medium price bracket. Sheepskin is dyed to a wide variety of colors as well as being finished in attractive natural tones, and can be used for leather garments and is ideal for accessories. Sheepskin suede is of a particularly good quality, soft and velvety, and is usually used for better quality fashion clothes.

Cowhide is a much heavier leather and comes in two or three different thicknesses, the central area of the hide being the thickest. This is used for shoe soles, suitcases and anything which needs to wear well. The sides of these hides are thinner and are suitable for heavier weight garments, such as skirts and jerkins and shoe uppers.

Cowhide is also sold in "splits", which means that the skin has been split through its thickness into two layers. Splits are the cheapest kind of leather to buy, but are not very strong and shouldn't be used for articles where there is likely to be a strain on the leather—such as across the shoulders of a garment. It's perfectly suitable for accessories and is easily obtainable.

Calfskin, the smooth, beautiful leather used for good handbags and shoes, is available in different weights and finishes and is more expensive than sheepskin.

Among the fancy leathers are pigskins, goatskins, lizard and snakeskin and but these are generally rather difficult to obtain.

Leather and suede is sold by the square foot unless one is buying offcuts or scrap pieces. Skins are of an irregular shape with the legs and neck of the animal sticking out from the "body", but these are calculated in the given measurement.

## The basic tools

To make even quite simple things, a few basic tools are essential. The most important are a cutting board, a sharp leather knife and a good pair of scissors; ideally these should be leather shears but this isn't essential. A bone folder, which nowadays is sometimes made of plastic, is used for scoring lines on the leather and for smoothing and flattening edges. A skiving knife, available from craft shops, is invaluable where hems and turnings need to be as thin as possible. Useful adjuncts are an oilstone on which to keep the knife sharp, a leather punch for thonged articles, a stitch marking wheel and a stitch tool, which makes slits for the thread instead of holes. A steel ruler, a triangle and a compass are necessary for accurate measuring.

### Sewing leather and suede

Of the four basic methods of joining leather—glueing, lacing or thonging, machine-stitching and hand-sewing—the latter two are used most.

To sew leather by hand, both straight and curved needles, glover's needles (which have a sharp triangular point) and saddler's needles are used, depending on the item being stitched.

For sewing using a sewing machine, medium thick needles will be found to be the most satisfactory, and the size of stitch should be regulated to the thickness of the leather. For thick work, set the stitch large, and for fine leather the stitch can be relatively small. Suedes tend to drag when more than one thickness is going through the machine, and to correct this adjust the stitch to the next size up. The thread will sink into the suede anyway and the finished appearance should be satisfactory.

### Threads for leathercraft

Choose a thread suitable for the job in hand, determining the gauge for both appearance and performance. Whichever thread is chosen however, it must be waxed with beeswax or paraffin wax before use to prevent fraying and breaking. Heavier kinds of cotton, silk and nylon threads can be used for hand-sewing and for machine-stitching, providing that the machine needle is the right size. Linen thread is both decorative and strong for hand-sewing and is ideal for thin, supple leathers and suedes. Buttonhole silk is appropriate for gloves and bags, while bookbinder's thread and carpet yarn, available in different gauges, are very strong and are suitable for most types of leather. Saddler's thread is good for heavy duty articles.

### Preparing leather for joining.

Sewing leather by hand can be fairly hard work, and by piercing holes first the job is made much easier. For saddle stitch-
1722

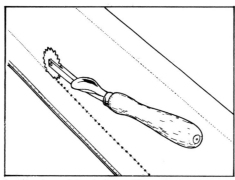

**6.** *Cutting leather thonging*

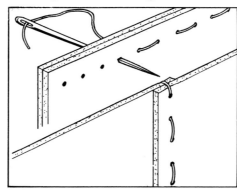

**2.** *The technique of skiving*

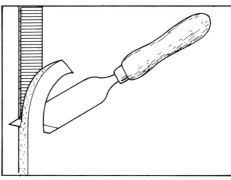

**3.** *Working running stitch*

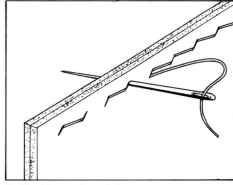

**4.** *Double running stitch*

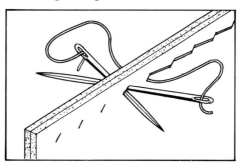

**5.** *Working saddle stitch*

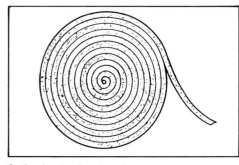

**1.** *Piercing with stitch marking wheel*

ing, pierce the holes with a sharp pointed awl but make sure that the holes are equidistant. Pierce along a ruler's edge or use a stitch marking wheel (diagram **1**).

For leathers and suedes which aren't too heavy, use the sewing machine without thread in the needle to pierce holes.

For lacing or thonging, holes are either punched or slit. Slit punches and pronged thonging tools can be purchased in craft shops; a plier-action punch is best for making round holes.

**Skiving.** Skiving is the term used for paring down the edges of leather and suede so that they can be more easily turned for glueing. Diagram **2** shows the technique. The knife is held at a very tight angle against the wrong side of the leather and guided toward the body and outward.

### Stitching seams by hand

There are three methods of stitching seams by hand, these are:

**Running stitch.** This is used for joining ordinary seams and lapped seams. If thongs are being used for stitching, punch holes first in the leather. On lightweight leathers and suedes sew with a glover's needle. For heavier leathers, pierce holes and sew with a saddler's needle (diagram **3**).

**Double running stitch.** This gives a much stronger join and has something of the appearance of saddle stitching. Sew the seam once, using a gloving needle and a single running stitch. Then sew back the other way using an ordinary needle. The change of needles is necessary because if a gloving needle were used for the second stitching, the spear-like point would cut the first stitches (diagram **4**).

**Saddle stitching.** For this attractive finish, first wax the thread. Beeswax is used by professional workers but paraffin candle wax will do quite well. Pierce holes at a slight angle and then work as shown in diagram **5**. Two needles are used simultaneously to pull threads through and it is important to make uniform stitches.

▲ *This beautiful patent leather clutch bag can also be made in soft calf or suede*

### Thonging and lacing
Leather thonging can be purchased but it is quite easy to cut one's own. Diagram **6** shows the method.

### Glueing
There are good leather glues available from craft shops in both tubes and jars. Tubes are useful for edges and small areas; a jar with a brush is more satisfactory for larger areas. Rubber cement and latex based adhesives are good because they will rub off without leaving a stain.
Glueing is mostly used for attaching lining leathers to surface leathers and for putting on decorative leather edgings and bindings.

## Making a clutch bag

Patent leather has been used to make the bag illustrated, but any kind of leather or suede can be used instead. The pattern is based on very simple principles and can be adapted to make a coin purse, a tobacco pouch or a simple brief case.

Copy the diagram onto squared paper. Decide whether you are going to skive the edges so that they can be turned in for the same finish as the bag illustrated. If you decide not to attempt this kind of finish, the edges can be left raw. The line for cutting leather for a raw edged finish is colored. This is also the cutting line for the lining.
When the pattern is outlined on the squared paper cut out the pieces, main bag and gussets, in heavy paper and take these with you to a leather supplier to choose a skin. Choose a lining skin, called a "skiver" at the same time.

### Cutting out
Lay the pattern pieces on the skin so that the best area of leather is used for the flap. The paper pattern can be kept in position by sticking it to the leather with one or two pieces of clear tape. Mark around the pattern carefully with a pencil using a ruler. It is worth stressing at this point that possible difficulties will be

minimized if three rules are observed:
1. Cut out the paper pattern carefully.
2. Mark the pattern carefully on the skin.
3. Be really accurate in cutting out the leather.
Skive the edges of the leather at this point if this is the technique you are following.

### Interlining and pocket
Cut three pieces of cardboard interlining to the measurements given on the diagram and glue them to the wrong side of the leather, making sure that the edges are absolutely parallel. This is important if the bag is to fold properly. If a fastening is being used, this is the point at which the plates of the fastening are inserted. Snap fasteners can be used instead if preferred. Turn the skived edges of the bag flap and front edge (A-B-C-D and F-G in the diagram). Snip into the turnings $\frac{1}{2}$ inch where the top edge of the gusset will lie (D-d and A-a). Turn in and stick down the top edges of the gusset pieces too. Leave to dry.

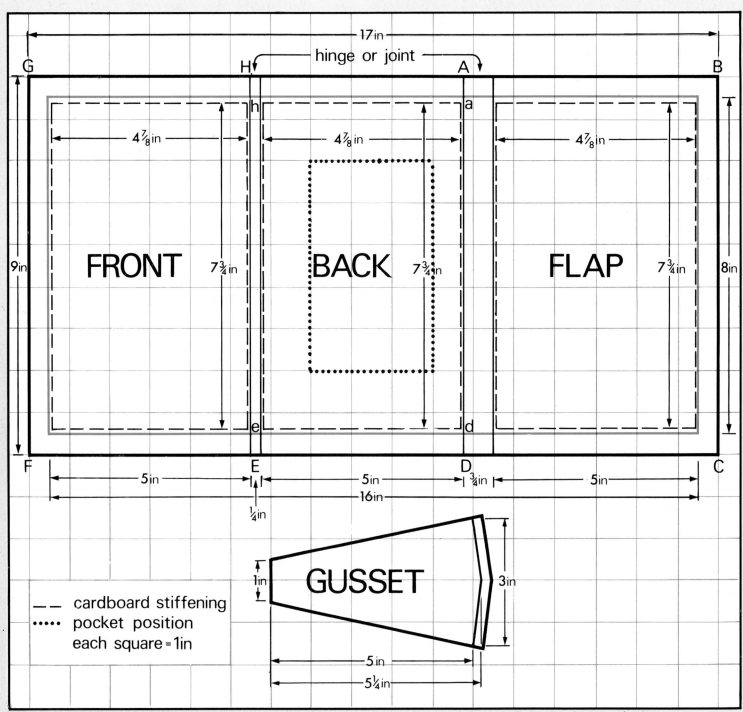

17in

hinge or joint

G H A B

$4\frac{7}{8}$in $4\frac{7}{8}$in $4\frac{7}{8}$in

FRONT $7\frac{3}{4}$in BACK $7\frac{3}{4}$in FLAP $7\frac{3}{4}$in

9in 8in

e d

F E D C

5in 5in $\frac{3}{4}$in 5in

16in

$\frac{1}{4}$in

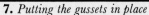

1in GUSSET 3in

−− cardboard stiffening
•••• pocket position
each square = 1in

5in
$5\frac{1}{4}$in

▲ *Plan your patterns for the clutch bag and lining from this diagram*

**7.** *Putting the gussets in place*

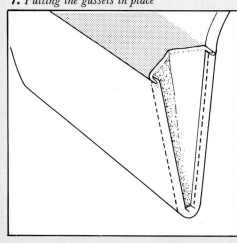

Fold the pocket piece in half as indicated and glue the two sides together to make a piece measuring 5 inches by 3 inches.

Meanwhile, cut out the bag lining from the lining fabric and lining for the gusset pieces, using the pattern.

When the pocket piece is dry, lightly stick it in position on the lining as indicated in the diagram and then machine stitch in position on three sides.

**Attaching the lining**

The lining is now glued to the outside leather, onto the surface of the cardboard interlining, and the gusset lining pieces are

also glued to the gusset pieces. Turn in the edges of lining as you work and smooth it down using the bone folder. When everything is dry, stitch the top edges of the two gusset pieces. Then machine stitch the top edge of the bag (G-F) and all around the flap (ABCD).

Turn the skived edges of the gusset pieces to the right side and turn the skived edges of the bag along lines GHA and FED to the wrong side. Snip at E-e and H-h. Glue and then stitch the gussets into place (diagram **7**). If it seems difficult to machine stitch the gussets, they can be sewn by hand.

▲ *A simple belt, a beautiful buckle*
▼ *Ways with bright suede*

▲ *Make this gay patchwork jerkin in diamond shapes. Cut a template first and cut sufficient pieces from scraps of suede. Cut out the garment pieces from heavy cotton (use a commercial paper pattern for a jerkin). Lightly glue the diamond shapes in position, just touching. Use a latex adhesive. When the glue is dry, machine stitch the diamond shapes into position, using a zigzag stitch. Make the garment as instructed in the pattern.*

▲ *Simple bag and belt in appliqué*
▼ *Belts and purses to make*

▼ *A quick belt to make in leather or suede. Cut out several shapes and link to waist measurement*

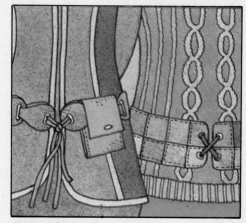

*Fasten with buckle or thong.*

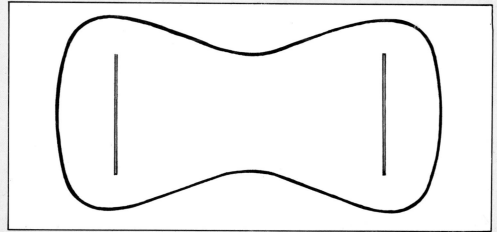

# Knitting pattern/chevron stripes for children

This children's outfit has back and front panels of chevron stripes. The contrast color continues in the hat and mitten edges.

## Sizes
Directions are for 24in chest. The figures in brackets [ ] refer to the 26, 28, and 30in sizes respectively.

**Pullover.** Length, 14[16½:19: 21½]in.
Sleeve seam, 11[12½:14:15½]in.
**Pants.** Inside leg, 12[15: 18:21]in.
**Mittens.** Length, 7[8½]in.
**Hat.** To fit average head.

### Gauge
5 sts and 6½ rows to 1in over st st worked on No.7 needles.

## Materials
Knitting Worsted 4 oz skeins
**Pullover.** 3[3:4:4] skeins main color, navy, A
2 skeins contrast, orange, B
**Pants.** 3[3:3:4] skeins main color, A
**Hat and mittens.** 1[1:2:2] skeins main color, A
1 skein contrast, B
One pair No. 5 needles (or Canadian No. 8)
One pair No. 7 needles (or Canadian No. 6)
Waist length elastic for pants

## Pullover back

### First side
Using No.5 needles and A, cast on 69[73:81:85] sts.
**1st row** K1, *P1, K1, rep from * to end.
**2nd row** P1, *K1, P1, rep from * to end.
Rep these two rows for 1½in, ending with 1st row.
**Next row** *Rib 2[2:3:3], K up 1 (inc), rep from * 4 times more, rib to last 10[10:15:15] sts, **K up 1, rib 2[2:3:3], rep from ** 4 times more. 79[83:91:95] sts.
Change to No.7 needles.
**Next row** K17[19:21:23], turn and cast on one st.
Continue on these 18[20:22: 24] sts in st st until work

measures 8½[10½:12½:14½]in from beg. End with a P row.

### Shape armhole
At arm edge, bind off on every other row 5 sts; then 3 sts; then 2 sts.
At armhole edge, K2 tog on every other row twice.
Continue without shaping on rem 6[8:10:12] sts until armhole measures 5½[6:6½: 7]in, ending with a P row.

### Shape armholes
Bind off 3[4:5:6] sts at beg of next row.
P 1 row.
Bind off rem 3[4:5:6] sts.

### Second side
Return to sts which were left and with RS facing, slip the first 45[45:49:49] sts onto a spare needle, attach yarn, cast on one st, K to end.
Continue on these 18[20:22: 24] sts to correspond to first side, reversing shaping.

### Center panel
Using No.7 needles and A, with RS facing, work over the center 45[45:49:49] sts as follows:
**1st row** Rib 4. Turn.
**2nd row** Rib 3, work into front, back, then front again of next st—called inc 2—.

**3rd row** Rib 10. Turn.
**4th row** Rib 9, inc 2.
**5th row** Rib 16. Turn.
**6th row** Rib 15, inc 2.
**7th row** Rib 22. Turn.
**8th row** Rib 21, inc 2.
**9th row** Rib 26. Turn.
**10th row** Rib 25, inc 2.
Break off yarn.
Slip all sts onto right-hand needle, attach yarn and with WS facing, beg at left side, rep 1st to 10th rows as above. Break off yarn and slip all sts back onto left-hand needle. 65[65:69:69] sts.
With RS facing and using B, continue as follows:
**1st row** K.

1726

**2nd row** Inc 2, rib 28[28:30:30], K3 tog, P1, K3 tog tbl, rib 28[28:30:30], inc 2.

**3rd row** Rib.

Rep 2nd and 3rd rows 3 times more, then 2nd row once.**

Using A, rep from ** to **. Working alternately 10 rows B, 10 rows A, continue as before until work measures the same as side piece to beg of shoulder shaping, ending with 10th row of a stripe.

**Next row** With next color, K.

**Next row** Rib to 3 sts before center st, K3 tog, P1, K3 tog tbl, rib to end.

**Next row** Rib to end.

Rep last two rows 3 times more, then first row once. 45[45:49:49]sts.***

**Next row** With next color, K.

**Next row** P2 tog, rib to 3 sts before center st, K3 tog, P1, K3 tog tbl, rib to last 2 sts, P2 tog.

**Next row** Rib.

Rep last two rows until 9[9:7:7] sts rem.

**Next row** K1[1:0:0], K3 tog, P1, K3 tog tbl, K1[1:0:0]. Bind off.

## Front

Work as given for Back to *** Bind off.

## Sleeves

Using No.5 needles and A, cast on 35[37:39:41] sts and work in rib as on Back for 2[2¼:2¼:2½]in, ending with 2nd row, inc one st in center of last row and one st at each end. 38[40:42:44] sts.

Change to No.7 needles. Beg with a K row, continue in st st, inc one st at each end of 3rd and every following 8th row until there are 52[54:58:60] sts.

Continue without shaping until sleeve seam measures 11[12½:14:15½]in from beg, ending with a P row.

### Shape cap

Bind off 5 sts at beg of next 2 rows.

K2 tog at each end of next and every other row until 26 sts rem.

Bind off 2 sts at beg of next 6 rows, then 3 sts at beg of next 2 rows.

Bind off rem 8 sts.

## Neckband

Join side panels to center Front and Back panels. Join right shoulder seam.

Using No.5 needles and A, pick up and K71[75:79:83] sts around neck.

Beg with second rib row, work in rib as at beg of Back for 4[4½:4½:5]in. Bind off loosely in rib.

## Pants right leg

Using No.5 needles and A, cast on 37[41:45:49] sts and work in rib as on Back of Pullover for 1¼in, ending with a second row.

Change to No.7 needles. Beg with a K row, continue in st st as follows:

**1st row** K9[10:11:12], sl 1, K17[19:21:23], sl 1, K9[10:11:12].

**2nd row** P.

Rep these two rows 2[3:4:5] times more.

**Next row** K2, *K up 1, K7[8:9:10], sl 1, K7[8:9:10], K up 1*, K3, rep from * to *, K2.

Keeping the continuity of the sl sts, work 5[7:9:11] rows.

**Next row** K2, *K up 1, K8[9:10:11], sl 1, K8[9:10:11], K up 1, *K3, rep from * to *, K2.

Continue inc in this way on every 6th[8th:10th:12th] rows until there are 77[81:85:89] sts.

Continue without shaping until work measures 12[15:18:21] in from beg, ending with a P row.

### Shape crotch

Bind off 4 sts at beg of next 2 rows, then 3 sts at beg of next row.

P 1 row.

**Next row** K2, K2 tog, K to last 4 sts, K2 tog tbl, K2.

Continue dec in this way on following 4th row, then on every following 4th[4th:6th:6th] row until 58[60:62:64] sts rem.

Continue without shaping until work measures 7½[8:8½:9]in from beg of crotch shaping, ending with a K row.

### Shape back

**Next row** P to last 32[32:36:36] sts, turn and K to end.

**Next row** P to last 36[36:40:40] sts, turn and K to end.

Continue working 4 sts less on every other row 3[3:4:4] times more.

**Next row** P across all sts, dec one st at end of row. 57[59:61:63] sts.

Change to No.5 needles. Continue in rib as at beg for 1¼in. Bind off in rib.

## Left leg

Work as for right Leg, reversing all shaping.

## Hat

Using No.5 needles and B, cast on 95[99:103:107] sts and work in rib as before for 1[1¼:1½:1¾]in, ending with a second row.

Change to No.7 needles and A.

**Next row** K5[2:4:6], * K up 1, K5, rep from * 16[18:18:18] times, K up 1, K5[2:4:6]. 113[119:123:127] sts.

Continue in rib until work measures 6½[7:7½:8]in from beg, ending with a WS row.

**Next row** K1, *K2 tog, rep from * to end. 57[60:62:64] sts.

**Next row** P.

**Next row** K1[0:0:0], *K2 tog, rep from * to end. 29[30:31:32] sts.

Break off yarn, thread through sts, draw up and fasten off securely.

## Mittens

Using No.5 needles and B, cast on 46[55] sts.

**1st row** K1, *P2, K1, rep from * to end.

**2nd row** P1, *K2, P1, rep from * to end.

Rep these two rows for 1¾in, ending with a second row.

**Next row** K1, *P2 tog, K1, rep from * to end. 31[37] sts.

Continue in K1, P1 rib until work measures 2¾[3¼]in, ending with a WS row.

Break off B.

Change to No.7 needles and attach A.

Work 4 rows st st.

**Next row** K15[18], K up 1, K1, K up 1, K15[18].

**Next row** P.

**Next row** K15[18], K up 1, K3, K up 1, K15[18].

Continue inc in this way on every other row 3[5] times more, ending with a P row.

**Next row** K24[31], turn, cast on one st.

**Next row** P10[14], turn, cast on one st.

**Next row** K11[15], turn.

Continue on these sts for thumb for 1[1½]in, ending with a P row.

**Next row** K1, *K2 tog, rep from * to end.

Break off yarn, thread through sts, draw up and fasten off. Join thumb seam.

Return to where work was left, attach yarn and K up 1 from base of thumb seam, K to end.

Continue on these 31[37] sts until work measures 6½[8]in from beg, ending with a P row.

**Next row** K1, *P1, K1, rep from * to end.

**Next row** P1, *K1, P1, rep from * to end.

**Next row** K1, *K2 tog, rep from * to end. 16[19] sts.

**Next row** P.

**Next row** K0[1], *K2 tog, rep from * to end. 8[10] sts.

Break off yarn, thread through sts, draw up and fasten off securely.

## Finishing

Press work with a warm iron under a damp cloth, omitting ribbing.

**Pullover.** Join left shoulder seams and neckband. Sew in sleeves. Join side and sleeve seams. Press all seams.

**Pants.** Join center front and back seams. Join leg seams. Sew elastic inside waistband with casing-stitch. Press all seams.

**Hat.** Join and press seam. Make pompon in two colors and sew to top.

**Mittens.** Join and press seam.

# Stitchery pattern/pattern for furnishings

The design for this richly decorated table runner is embroidered in two simple stitches using white yarn on a blue background to give a dramatic effect. This interesting design would also make a good inner and outer border decoration for a tablecloth, as a border on a curtain or worked in vertical bands. The design could be easily adapted for use on a pillow or to decorate a drum shaped lampshade.

To make this table runner measuring 14 inches wide by 50 inches long you will need:
- ☐ ½yd 59 inch wide even-weave linen with 21 threads to 1 inch, blue
- ☐ D.M.C. Pearl Cotton No.8, 3 balls
- ☐ Sewing thread to match linen
- ☐ Crewel needle No.16

## Method

With basting stitches mark the center of the fabric vertically and horizontally following the grain of the fabric. Work the design from the chart over two threads of fabric each way. The main part of the design is worked in cross-stitch and the fine lines in Holbein or double running stitch. Work twenty-one complete repeats of the design down the center along the length of the cloth. Finish the edges of the runner with a 1 inch deep hem, mitering the corners neatly.

▲ *The working chart for the upper half of the design*
*The table runner embroidered in cross-stitch and Holbein stitch* ► *Ways with the pattern*▼

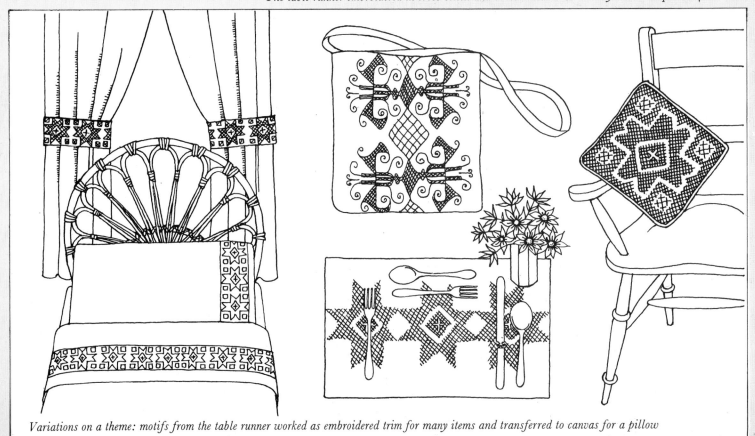

*Variations on a theme: motifs from the table runner worked as embroidered trim for many items and transferred to canvas for a pillow*

1729

# Stitchery design/metal thread embroidery

This chapter on metal thread embroidery illustrates some of the different effects which can be achieved by varying the threads and the techniques of applying them.

Although gold threads are rich and exciting to work with, silver and silver Lurex threads produce embroidery with a cool and exquisite look.

## Uses

Metal thread embroidery is traditionally associated with ecclesiastical work as a decoration for copes, miters, altar frontals, pulpit falls and prayer book covers, but in modern embroidery it is used for wall panels, and as a decoration for lids of fabric jewelry boxes.

On fashion garments metal thread embroidery adds luxurious richness, and will not cause cleaning problems as a variety of washable Lurex yarns are available.

## Fir cone

The background fabric is a cotton/synthetic mixture in dark brown. The applied fabrics are Japanese silk in bronze, gold kid in a variety of tones, and gloving leathers in browns. The metal threads used are Japanese gold, pearl purl, Lurex in antique gold and gold fingering knitting yarn. The Japanese silk was applied first, couched down with Japanese gold and Lurex. Shapes cut from leather and gold kid form cone seed detail. Couched gold threads and gold fingering knitting yarn are used for finer design lines.

## Tree bark

The background fabric used here is natural colored burlap, and the applied fabric is gold orion cloth which resembles kid. The raised, padded sections were worked first. Several layers of felt in varying sizes were stitched in place beginning with the smallest and finishing with the largest, giving a smooth, rounded padding. The orion cloth was then stitched down over the padding. The textured stitchery is a combination of gold and lurex threads couched down in vertical flowing lines to form rhythm in the design.

## Silver on blue

This sampler is worked on a slub textured home furnishing fabric, using a variety of materials in tones of silver. Narrow silver ribbon is crumpled in a random fashion and tiny matte, silver beads are stitched into the folds. Silver checkered purl, cut in lengths, is applied in small loops. Finer silver and Lurex threads and pure silk lightly scatter the background in the form of small star stitches and random crossed threads to contrast with the heavier textures. The circles of silver kid make interesting focal highlights.

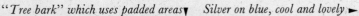

▼ *The design entitled "fir cone" worked in gold kid and leather*    *"Tree bark" which uses padded areas*▼    *Silver on blue, cool and lovely* ►

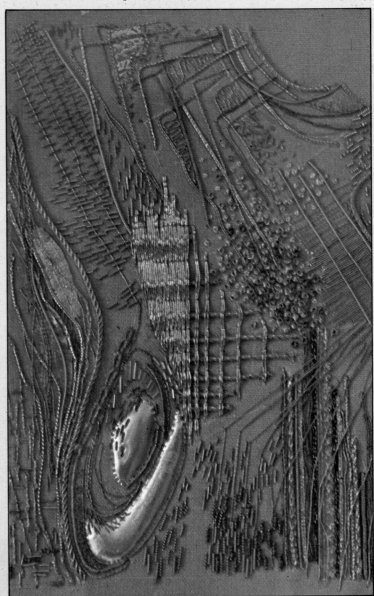

# Home crochet/bedspread for an heirloom

Here is the pattern for a beautiful bedspread that you will be proud to hand on to your children's children! This pretty bedspread is crocheted in knitting cotton, and can be plain or colored as desired. Three sizes are given, but as the pattern consists of one easy-to-work motif repeated over and over again, the bedspread can be adapted to fit a bed of any dimensions.

## Sizes

**Single bed size.** About 56in by 102in.
**Double bed size.** About 70in by 112in.
**King bed size.** About 77in by 116in.

The figures in brackets [ ] refer to the double bed and king bed sizes respectively.

**Gauge**
One motif measures 3½in.

## Materials

Coats & Clark's O.N.T. Speed-Cro-Sheen 39[54:60] 100 yd balls
One No. D (3.00 mm) crochet hook

## Motif

Using No.D hook, ch8, join with a ss into first ch to form ring.
**1st round** Work 24sc into ring, join with a ss into first sc.
**2nd round** *1sc into next sc, ch3, skip 1sc, rep from * 11 times more, join with a ss into first sc. 12 sps.
**3rd round** Ss into each of next 2ch, 1sc into sp, *ch5, 1sc into next sp, ch3, 1sc into next sp, rep from * 4 times more, ch5, 1sc into next sp, ch3, ss into first sc.
**4th round** Ss into next ch5 sp, ch4, 6tr into same sp, ch3, 1sc into next ch3 sp, *ch3, 7tr into next sp, ch3, 1sc into next sp, rep from * 4 times more, ch3, ss into 4th of 4ch.
**5th round** 1sc into same place as ss, 1sc into next tr, ch2, 1sc into each of next 3tr, ch2, 1sc into each of next 2tr, ch4, *1sc into each of next 2tr, ch2, 1sc into each of next 3tr, ch2, 1sc into each of next 2tr, ch4, rep from * 4 times more, join with a ss into first sc.

## Second motif

Work rounds 1-4 as for first motif.
**5th round** Work as given for first motif until 5grs have been worked over, 1sc into each of next 2sc, ch1, insert hook into ch2 loop on first motif, yoh, pull yarn through, ch1, 1sc into each of next 3tr, ch1, insert hook into next ch2 loop on first motif, yoh and pull yarn through, ch1, 1sc into each of next 2tr, ch4, ss into first sc.

## Finishing

**1st row** Join 16[20:22] motifs.
**2nd row** Using the same method join first group to first motif of previous row, second group to second motif of previous row. On all but the first motif, the sixth group is joined to the previous motif on the same row. In this way the second row is positioned alternately to the first.
Continue in this way, joining by the same method on the required groups, until 29[32: 33] rows have been joined.

▼ *Close-up detail of a single motif from the bedspread illustrated left*

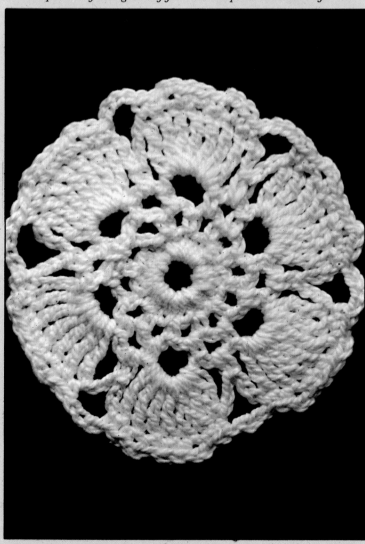

▼ *Various ways of using the motif in a bedroom scheme*

# Home crochet/window filigree

Crochet window filigrees are a charming idea, popular in Scandinavia where they originated, probably inspired by the patterns of magnified snowflakes. This pretty design can be used in other ways around the home. It would make a beautiful table mat, with the edges left irregular. Alternatively, you could add an edge by working a chain instead of using a hoop, and working single crochet into each chain all around.

## Size
About 16in diameter.

### Gauge
7dc and 2 rows to 1in worked with No.D crochet hook.

## Materials
J. & P. Coats
"Knit-Cro-Sheen"
1 (175 yd) ball
One No. D (3.00 mm) crochet hook
16 in diameter metal or plastic hoop

## Filigree
Ch4, join with a ss to form a ring.

**1st round** *Ch15, ss into ring, rep from * 3 times more.

**2nd round** Into each of the 4 loops just made work 30dc.

**3rd round** Ss over first 7dc of first loop, 1sc into next dc, *(ch7, skip 2dc, 1sc into next dc) 5 times, ch5, 1sc into 8th dc of next loop, rep from * 3 times more, ending last rep with ss into first sc of round.

**4th round** Ss over first 3ch, 1sc into loop, (ch7, 1sc into next ch7 loop) to end, ending with ch7, ss into first sc of round.

**5th round** Ss over first 3ch, 1sc into loop, *(ch9, 1sc into next loop) 3 times, ch3, 1sc into next loop, ch10, ss into last sc worked, 21dc into the ch10 loop just made, ss again into the same sc, ch3, 1sc into next loop, rep from * 3 times more, ending with ss into first sc.

**6th round** Ss over first 4ch, *6sc into loop, (6sc, ch2, 6sc) into next loop, 6sc into next loop, ch5, 1sc into 8th dc around ring, (ch5, skip 2dc, 1sc into next dc) twice, ch5, rep from * 3 times more, ending with ss into first sc.

**7th round** Ch9, *(1sc, ch2, 1sc) into ch2 loop, ch5, (1dc, ch3, 1dc) into last of 6sc in next loop, ch5, skip next loop, (1sc into next loop, ch5) twice, (1dc, ch3, 1dc) into first of 6sc, ch5, rep from * 3 times more, ending with 1dc into first st, ch3, ss into 4th of first 9ch.

**8th round** Ch5, *(1dc, ch3, 1dc) into ch2 loop, (1dc, ch5, 1dc) into next dc, ch3, 1dc into next dc, ch7, skip next loop, 1sc into next loop, ch7, 1dc into next dc, ch3, (1dc, ch5, 1dc) into next dc, rep from * 3 times more, ending with ch3, 1dc into first st, ch5, ss into 4th of 5ch.

**9th round** Ss into next ch5 loop, ch3, 4dc into this loop, **(ch3, 1dc into next loop) twice, ch3, 9dc into next loop, ch2, 9dc into next loop, (ch3, 1dc into next loop) twice, ch3, *5dc into next loop, rep from ** twice more, then rep from ** to *, ending with ss into 3rd of 3ch.

**10th round** Ch3, 1dc into each of next 4dc, **(ch3, 1dc into next dc) twice, ch3, 1dc into each of next 4dc, ch2, skip 1dc, 1dc into each of next 4dc, 4dc into ch2 sp, 1dc into each of next 4dc, ch2, skip 1dc, 1dc into each of next 4dc, (ch3, 1dc into next dc) twice, ch3*, 1dc into each of next 5dc, rep from ** twice more, then rep from ** to *, ss into 3rd of 3ch.

**11th round** Ch4, (1dc into next dc, ch1) 4 times, **ch2, (1dc into next dc, ch3) 3 times, (1dc, ch1) 4 times into ch2 sp, then 1dc into the same sp, skip 4dc, (1dc into next dc, ch1) 3 times, 1dc into next dc, (1dc, ch1) 4 times into ch2 sp, then 1dc into the same sp, ch3, skip 3dc, (1dc into next dc, ch3) 3 times*, (1dc into next dc, ch1) 5 times, rep from ** twice more, then rep from ** to *, ss into 3rd of 5ch.

**12th round** Ch5, (1dc into next dc, ch2) 4 times, **ch1, (1dc into next dc, ch3) 3 times, (1dc into next dc, ch2) 4 times, 1dc into each of next 2dc, ch2, (1dc into next dc, ch2) twice, 1dc into next 2dc, (ch2, 7dc into next dc) 4 times, ch3, (1dc into next dc, ch3) 3 times*, (1dc into next dc, ch2) 5 times, rep from ** twice more, then rep from ** to *, ss into 3rd of 5ch.

**13th round** Ss into next sp, ch3, 4dc into this sp, **ch2, skip 1sp, 1dc into next dc, ch2, skip 1sp, 5dc into next sp, (ch3, 1dc into next dc) 3 times, ch3, 5dc into ch2 sp, skip 1sp, (ch2, 1dc into next dc) twice, ch2, skip 1sp, 1dc between next 2dc, ch2, skip 1sp, 5dc into next sp, ch2, skip 1sp, 1dc between next 2dc, (ch2, 1dc into next dc) twice, ch2, skip 1sp, 5dc into next sp, (ch3, 1dc into next dc) 3 times, ch3*, 5dc into ch2 sp, rep from ** twice more, then rep from ** to *, ss into 3rd of 3ch.

**14th round** Ch5, **5dc into ch2 sp, ch2, 5dc into next sp, skip 4dc, (ch3, 1dc into next dc) 3 times, ch3, skip 1sp,* (5dc into next sp, ch2) twice, skip 1sp, 1dc into next dc, ch2, skip 1sp*, rep from * to * once more, 5dc into next sp, ch2, 5dc into next sp, ch3, skip 1sp, (1dc into next dc, ch3) 3 times, rep from ** 3 times more but ending last rep with (1dc into next dc, ch3) twice instead of 3 times, ss into 3rd of 5ch. Fasten off.

## Finishing

Work in blanket stitch all around the metal hoop, covering it closely.
Pin out the filigree to size and press under a wet cloth using a hot iron. Leave to dry.
Sew the filigree to the hoop as illustrated.
Crochet a chain the required length and sew to hoop, forming a loop at one end to use for hanging.

*The filigree stitched to a metal hoop to hang in a window* ▶

1735

# Tailoring six

## A. Making a step collar

The collar of a coat should be smooth and well fitted, so great care must be taken not to distort it when stitching and pressing. The collar is sewn to the coat by hand to insure a perfect fit.

### The under collar
Stitch the center back seam. Trim the seam allowance to $\frac{1}{4}$ inch and press open.
**1.** Working on the under collar canvas, trim the center back seam allowance to $\frac{1}{4}$ inch, overlap on sewing line and stitch.
**2.** Lay the canvas to the wrong side of the under collar with center backs matching. Pin along the crease line, then run a taut thread along the crease line in matching thread.
**3.** The crease line on the collar divides the stand from the fall.
**4.** Fold the under collar on the crease line with the canvas side up, and pad stitch the fall, keeping within the stitching lines all around. Work with the crease line away from you and work up and down in staggered lines.
**5.** Similarly, pad stitch the stand, again working with the crease line away from you.

### Pressing the collar pieces
To fit the coat correctly the under and top collar pieces need to be pressed and molded before being stitched together.
**6.** Lay the under collar, right side down, on an ironing board. Using a damp cloth press the fall, gently pulling the outer edge of the collar slightly, just above the shoulder position. Always pull toward the center back as the center back must not be stretched. The edge should not be stretched more than $\frac{1}{2}$ inch.
**7.** Repeat for the stand.
**8.** Turn the under collar right side up and lay it flat on an ironing board with the stand folded over on the crease line. Using a damp cloth press firmly without stretching.
**9.** While the under collar is still damp, curve it around a dessert mold, with the stand turned in, to dry into a curve.

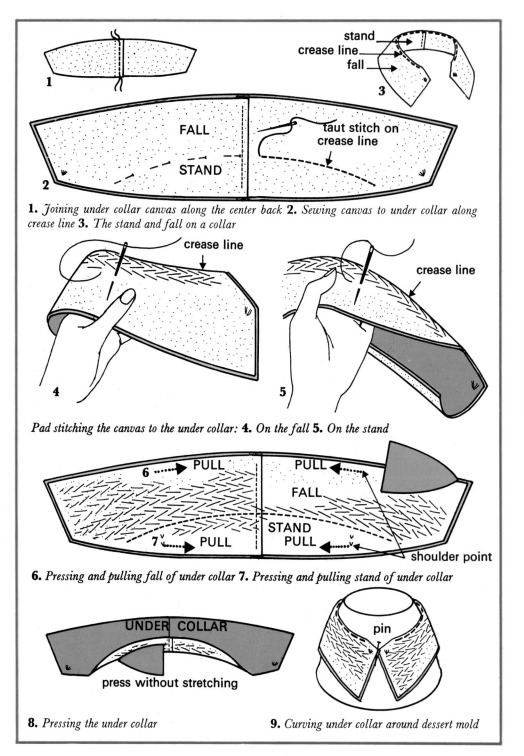

**1.** *Joining under collar canvas along the center back* **2.** *Sewing canvas to under collar along crease line* **3.** *The stand and fall on a collar*

*Pad stitching the canvas to the under collar:* **4.** *On the fall* **5.** *On the stand*

**6.** *Pressing and pulling fall of under collar* **7.** *Pressing and pulling stand of under collar*

**8.** *Pressing the under collar*

**9.** *Curving under collar around dessert mold*

Prepare the top collar similarly, but turning the stand under.

### Stitching the collar
**10.** Working on the under collar, trim the canvas to just inside the stitching line.
**11.** Check that the under collar fits neatly into the neckline with the ends matching.
**12.** Place the top and under collar pieces together, with right sides facing. Baste along crease line and along outside and step edges.
**13.** Stitch, layer seams and snip corners.

**14.** Turn the collar to the right side and work the corners or curves into a good shape. Working on the underside, baste along the stitched edges keeping the seam rolled to the underside. Side stitch the seam edges to keep them in place.
**15.** Turn under the seam allowance on the neck edge of the under collar and baste. Snip into the neck edge seam allowance of the top collar at the shoulder points. Turn under the seam allowance from the front edges to the shoulder point as shown and baste.
Press the collar very carefully.

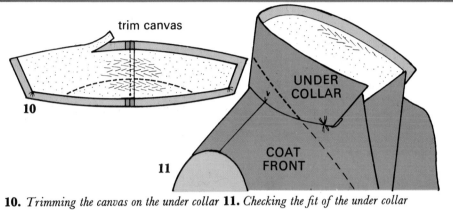

trim canvas

**10**

**11** UNDER COLLAR

COAT FRONT

**10.** *Trimming the canvas on the under collar* **11.** *Checking the fit of the under collar*

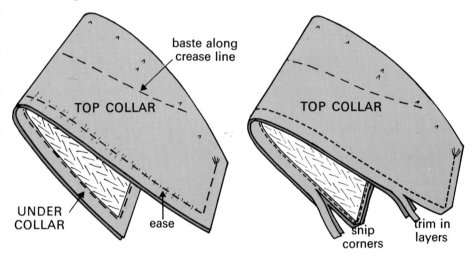

baste along crease line

TOP COLLAR

UNDER COLLAR

ease

TOP COLLAR

snip corners

trim in layers

**12.** *Basting top and under collars together*          **13.** *Stitched collar seams ready for turning*

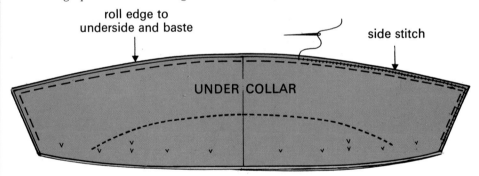

roll edge to underside and baste

side stitch

UNDER COLLAR

**14.** *The stitched edges of the turned collar basted and side stitched in place*

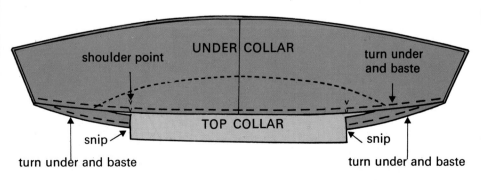

UNDER COLLAR

shoulder point

turn under and baste

TOP COLLAR

snip

snip

turn under and baste

turn under and baste

**15.** *Turning under and basting the neck edges of the collar ready for attaching to coat*

*Coat with step collar, Butterick pattern*

*Coat with fitted collar from Vogue Patterns*
*Coat with mandarin collar from Vogue Patterns*

## Attaching the collar to the coat

Lay the coat, right side up, over your knees with the neckline toward you.

**16.** Lay the under collar to the neck edge of the coat, right side up, with the folded edge of the undercollar meeting the sewing line of the coat neck edge. Carefully match the center backs, shoulder points and crease line. Pin along the neck edge distributing the ease evenly.

**17.** Fell the collar to the coat, starting at the center back and working to each end. Finish the ends off securely.

**18 a, b.** Still with the coat on your knees, turn the coat over to the wrong side. Pad stitch the end of the bridle firmly to the crease of the collar (**a**). Turn in the seam allowance of the facings along the neck edge in a smooth line and baste to coat (**b**).

**19.** Put the folded edges of the top collar to the folds of the facing. Using a draw stitch, draw the folds together making the stitches invisible (Tailoring 5, page 1716).

**20.** The raw edge at the back of the top collar is herringboned down as shown. This is eventually covered by the lining. Press the neck seam carefully over a ham.

## B. Making a fitted collar

**21.** A fitted collar is worked exactly as for the step collar. The crease line on a fitted collar runs from center front to center front as shown.

## C. Making a mandarin collar

Like the step collar, the mandarin collar is also attached to the coat by hand.

**22.** Cut a strip of wool and hair canvas to the shape of the collar without seam allowance. Catch stitch to the inside collar piece.

**23.** Place the collar pieces together, with right sides facing. Baste and stitch, starting and ending at the neck seamline.

**24.** Layer the seams and snip corners. Fold the neck seam allowances to the wrong side and baste.

Turn the collar to the right side, working corners into a good shape. Baste and press.

**25.** Sew the mandarin collar to the coat as for the step collar (figures **16, 17, 18,** and **19**), in the position indicated on the pattern, remembering that the under collar is now facing inward.

## D. Setting in the sleeves

The coat is now ready to have the sleeves set in.

### Pinning in the sleeves

Make sure that the sleeves are put into

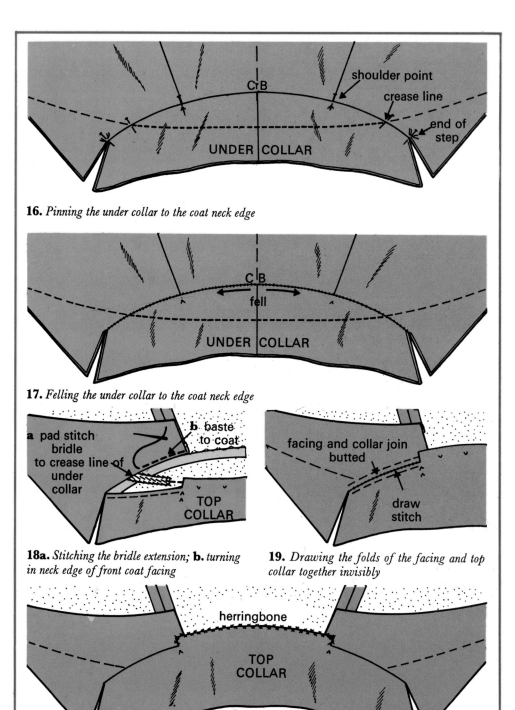

**16.** *Pinning the under collar to the coat neck edge*

**17.** *Felling the under collar to the coat neck edge*

**18a.** *Stitching the bridle extension;* **b.** *turning in neck edge of front coat facing*

**19.** *Drawing the folds of the facing and top collar together invisibly*

**20.** *The seam allowance at the back of the top collar herringboned to the coat*

their correct armholes. This might sound a silly thing to say but a mistake can easily be made.

**26.** Turn the coat wrong side out. Put the sleeve into the armhole with the right side of the sleeve facing right side of coat.
Working from inside the sleeve, pin all matching points as shown, incorporating any alterations made during the second fitting.

### Smooth fitted sleeve cap

**27.** Hold the coat with the armhole seam rolled back over the fingers. Pin away the ease between the pins already in place. Baste with small stitches.

### Gathered sleeve cap

**28.** Some fashion coats are being designed with a slight gather at the sleeve cap.
Run a gathering thread as shown in the pattern instructions. Pin in the sleeve as shown in figure **26**, then pull this thread until the sleeve cap fits the armhole.

**29.** Make sure that the gathers are even, then pin and baste with small stitches.

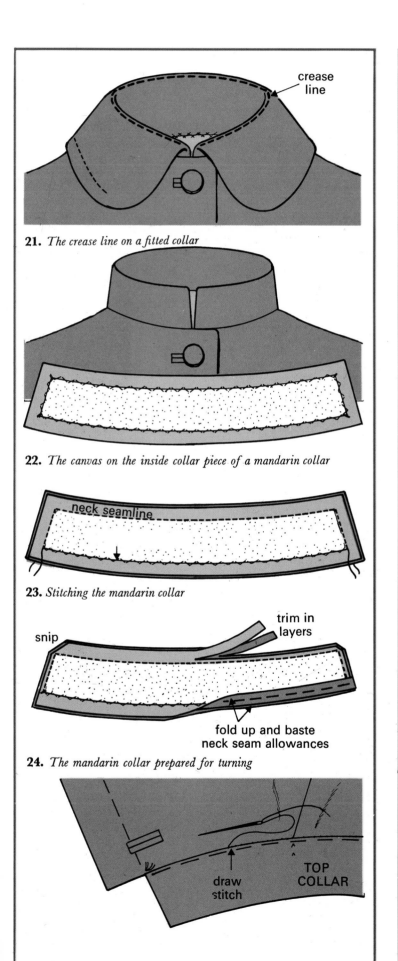

**21.** *The crease line on a fitted collar*

**22.** *The canvas on the inside collar piece of a mandarin collar*

neck seamline

**23.** *Stitching the mandarin collar*

snip

trim in layers

fold up and baste neck seam allowances

**24.** *The mandarin collar prepared for turning*

draw stitch

TOP COLLAR

**25.** *Stitching the mandarin collar to the coat*

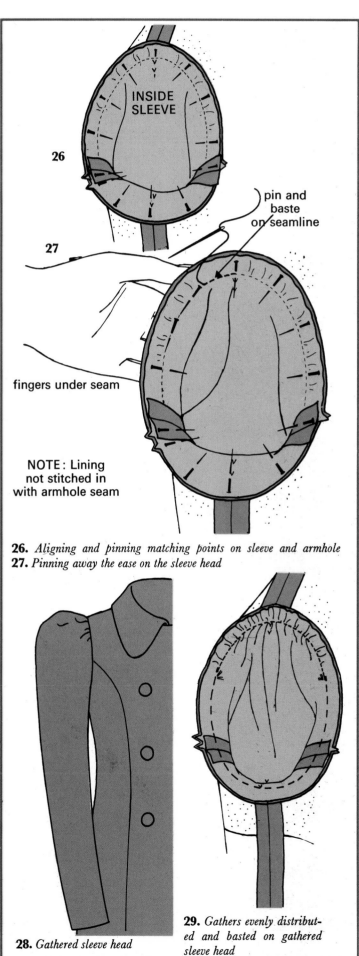

INSIDE SLEEVE

26

27

pin and baste on seamline

fingers under seam

NOTE: Lining not stitched in with armhole seam

**26.** *Aligning and pinning matching points on sleeve and armhole*
**27.** *Pinning away the ease on the sleeve head*

**28.** *Gathered sleeve head*

**29.** *Gathers evenly distribut- ed and basted on gathered sleeve head*

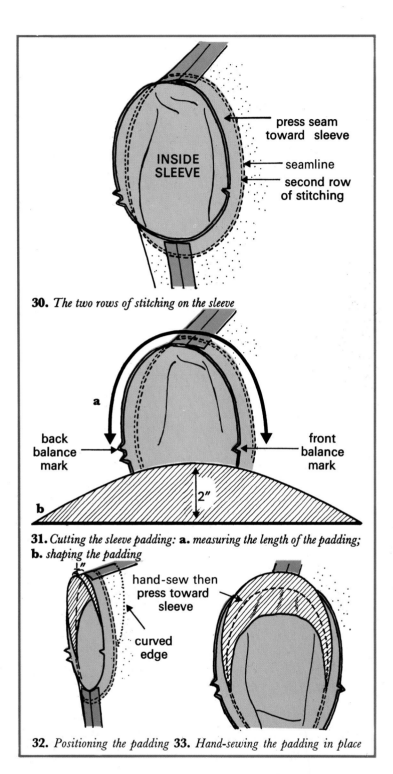

**30.** *The two rows of stitching on the sleeve*

**31.** *Cutting the sleeve padding:* **a.** *measuring the length of the padding;* **b.** *shaping the padding*

**32.** *Positioning the padding* **33.** *Hand-sewing the padding in place*

## E. The third fitting

Position shoulder pads if needed and put on the coat to have a final look at the sleeves. Ask a friend to help you as the hang of the sleeves alters with movement and you need to be perfectly still to get the correct set.

Also check that there is enough ease across the back when you make natural movements, such as sitting in a driving position, pushing a baby carriage, etc.

It is a good idea to give the length a final check too.

## F. Stitching in the sleeves

The sleeves can be machine-stitched or hand-sewn in place with a backstitch. Always work from inside the sleeve as you can control the fullness this way.

**30.** Make a second row of stitching in the seam allowance $\frac{1}{8}$ inch outside the first row. Without trimming the seam press it toward the sleeve, shrinking the sleeve seam carefully at the top.

### Sleeve cap padding

Padding the sleeve cap gives a slightly rounded look to a smooth cap and will support the shape of a gathered one.

**31a** and **b.** Measure the length over the shoulder from the back balance mark to the front balance mark (**a**). Cut two pieces of tailor's wadding to that length and shape as shown (**b**).

**32.** Place the curved side to the sleeve so that the padding extends $\frac{1}{4}$ inch at the sleeve cap.

**33.** Using matching thread, hand-sew the pad firmly in place on the second line of stitches, working through all thicknesses of the fabric.

# Crafts/dressing costume dolls

▲ *Note the detail of material and accessories in this Victorian dress.*

▲ *A copy of the costume worn by Dame Margot Fonteyn in "Firebird"*

## Choosing a theme for costume dolls

Dressing costume dolls is an appealing craft for anyone who likes to work in miniature and finds enjoyment in improvising for detailed effects. A collection can be built up according to one's particular interest: historical costumes provide an opportunity for working with rich fabrics, sequins and beads, while national costumes offer scope for embroidery. Theatrical costumes are another idea for a collection, choosing clothes worn by famous actors and actresses, or one might decide to build a collection of twentieth-century fashion.

## Selecting a suitable doll

It is important to choose dolls which can be obtained fairly easily, particularly when a collection is being started. Dolls with an adult look are essential—it is very difficult to make a baby doll look anything but a baby—and if special poses are required choose one with adjustable limbs. All the dressed dolls in this chapter are of one particular type, and it can be seen that they seem to take on different features once the costume is on them.

This particular make of doll is made in such a way that the arms, legs, and head can be easily removed to simplify dressing.

The Firebird is of the same make but with jointed limbs.

## Fabrics and effects

It is very important to use fabrics in scale with the doll. Look for fabrics with this clearly in mind. Small prints and fine weaves will give a dressed doll a more realistic look, and if the desired print isn't available use a plain fabric and paint the design. The Tudor doll's skirt has been treated in this way and it looks very effective. Fabrics can be painted with gold, silver, poster paints or inks after they have been constructed. Alter-

▲ *A pretty Swedish folk-costume with blouse and vest.*

▲ *A Regency outfit with a heavily trimmed hem.*

natively, felt pens or fabric paints can be used to paint the fabrics before they are made.

Short cuts can be used to achieve the final effect, such as glueing on details like sequins, jewels, feathers or trimmings, but use a good adhesive that will dry clear.

Search out and keep miniature trims of all kinds: broken necklaces for jewels, ribbon, lace edging, rouleau trimming and tiny buttons all help to build up the effect. Silver paper, foil, doilies in white, silver and gold, feathers, scraps of wool, pieces of tinsel, and even gift wrapping paper should be in your store of pieces.

Choose fabrics which do not fray easily wherever possible. Felt, of course, is good,

and so is Pellon interfacing; the latter can be painted or sprayed and is very good for making hats and other accessories. Don't, however, reject velvet, silk and satin as fabrics simply because they fray—they do add tremendous richness to costumes. Instead, handle these materials carefully and don't cut seams too finely.

**Ideas for costume and making patterns**

Once the collective theme has been decided on, try to find color pictures or drawings to work from. Study the reference carefully and get the essential line of the dress firmly in mind. One characteristic of the garment will stand

out—in the Tudor doll's costume, for instance, it is the sleeves. Try to find out what the back of the costume looks like—this is fairly important.

Cut patterns for the garment pieces in newspaper, pinning them onto the doll for fit, but remember to allow for seams. Costume dolls are rarely undressed so it isn't necessary to consider openings and fastenings.

Once sewing has started, it is usually easier to sew sections directly onto the doll. The Tudor costume was constructed bodice first, then the skirt, the ruff, and finally the sleeves. A better fit is achieved in this way and if one section is wrong it can easily be removed.

## Regency lady

The main characteristic of this period was the high waisted dress ending well above the ankles, heavily trimmed on the lower half of the skirt to emphasize the tubular look of the dress. It was slightly padded at the junction of the skirt and bodice at the back to make it stand away from the body.

Over the dress went either a dark colored Spencer jacket, as in our costume, or a coat that ended above the hemline. In summer, heavily fringed, patterned shawls were used indoors and out, and a high crowned hat or a turban was worn, usually richly trimmed. White or pink stockings and flat heelless slippers completed the outfit.

Draw the pattern pieces from the chart to make a paper pattern. Cut out the pieces. Choose a sprigged, dotted or plain pale cotton fabric for the main dress. Join the bodice at the side seams, and edge the neck and armholes by turning under a very small amount, slip stitching into place. Cut one skirt piece and join it at the back, leaving a one inch opening. Gather the skirt. Gather rows of fabric frills or lace or ribbon onto the skirt and hem the edge. Cut out the jacket sections in dark navy or black fabric, making the opening of the bodice in the front this time. Sew on thick embroidery thread or wool at the lines shown on the graph and lace at the lower cuff edge. Pin the sleeves into the bodice while it is flat, allowing the fullness to be at the top to get the delightful puffed effect.

Sew the sleeves in securely and then sew the side and underarm seam in one operation. The bottom band of the Spencer is put on like bias binding and slip stitched inside. The collar is made in the same way. Both garments can now be fastened onto the doll with small stitches using matching thread.

The bonnet is made from Pellon or felt. Join the crown back seam and stitch in the crown top, make small $\frac{1}{4}$ inch cuts $\frac{1}{2}$ inch apart on the bottom edge of the crown. This will allow it to sit on the brim without a clumsy seam. Stitch or glue in place. Sew lace around the brim and glue ribbon around the crown and brim junctions to cover the overlapping parts. Allow ends 3-4 inches long to tie under the chin. Glue feathers or flowers to the side of the bonnet.

## Tudor lady

This costume is copied from a portrait in the National Portrait Gallery in London, England. The ruff is made of Pellon and

▲ *A Tudor costume taken from a portrait in the National Portrait Gallery, London, England*

the headdress is made of Pellon covered in ribbon. Lace trim is glued on afterward. It is difficult to get fabric to pleat well in miniature, so it was important for this costume to get a good representation of the general line.

## Victorian lady

The fabric has to be constructed to scale for this costume and consists of lace ribbon over rayon. The skirt and blouse are made separately and joined on the doll. The jacket is a separately made garment and the brooch is a jet button. The hat is made of Pellon and the shoes have been painted with model paint.

## The Firebird

This costume was inspired by one worn by Dame Margot Fonteyn in the ballet "The Firebird". The feathers are hen feathers dyed in ink and sewn to the dress bodice. It was necessary to sew the doll's hair into a different style for this costume, and stage make-up has been painted onto her face.

## Swedish folk-costume

The blouse is made on the doll and the vest is separate. Motifs were cut from braid for the hat decoration. A crochet strip was worked for the hat.

1743

▼**CHART FOR REGENCY COSTUME**

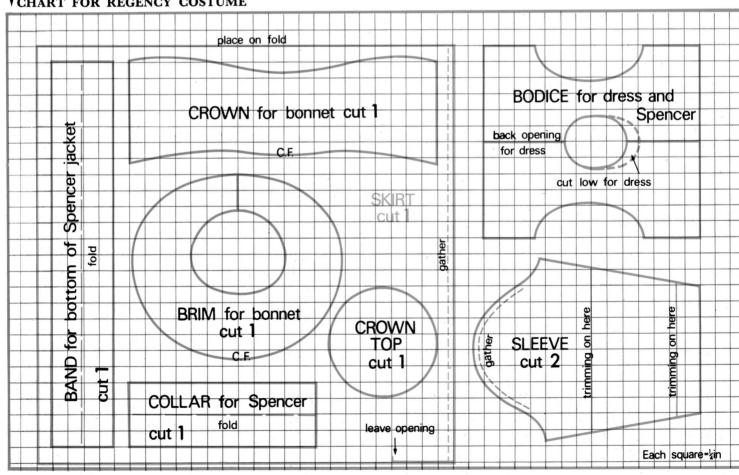

place on fold

BAND for bottom of Spencer jacket

fold

cut 1

CROWN for bonnet cut 1

C.F.

BRIM for bonnet
cut 1

C.F.

COLLAR for Spencer

cut 1     fold

SKIRT
cut 1

gather

CROWN
TOP
cut 1

leave opening

BODICE for dress and
Spencer

back opening
for dress

cut low for dress

gather

SLEEVE
cut 2

trimming on here

trimming on here

Each square=¼in

1744

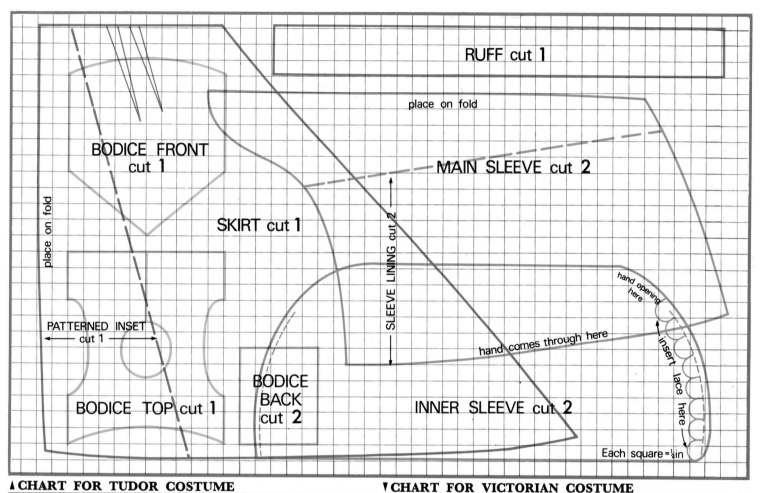

RUFF cut 1

place on fold

BODICE FRONT cut 1

place on fold

MAIN SLEEVE cut 2

SKIRT cut 1

SLEEVE LINING cut 2

hand opening here

insert lace here

PATTERNED INSET cut 1

hand comes through here

BODICE TOP cut 1

BODICE BACK cut 2

INNER SLEEVE cut 2

Each square = ¼in

▲ CHART FOR TUDOR COSTUME    ▼ CHART FOR VICTORIAN COSTUME

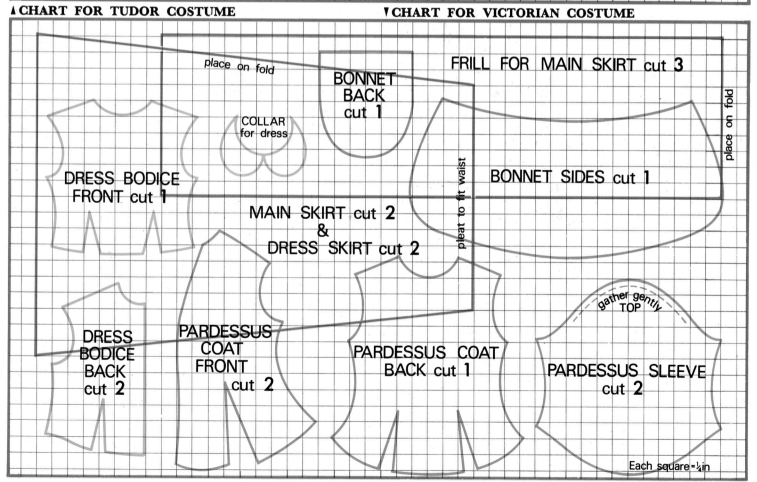

place on fold

BONNET BACK cut 1

FRILL FOR MAIN SKIRT cut 3

place on fold

COLLAR for dress

DRESS BODICE FRONT cut 1

BONNET SIDES cut 1

MAIN SKIRT cut 2 & DRESS SKIRT cut 2

pleat to fit waist

gather gently TOP

DRESS BODICE BACK cut 2

PARDESSUS COAT FRONT cut 2

PARDESSUS COAT BACK cut 1

PARDESSUS SLEEVE cut 2

Each square = ¼in

1746

# Knitting pattern/belted suit

The skirt of this elegant suit is knitted in stockinette stitch, and coordinates with a rib effect jacket that is three-quarter length.

## Sizes

Directions are for 32in bust. The figures in brackets [] refer to the 34, 36, 38 and 40in sizes respectively.
**Jacket.** Length, 29[29½:30: 30½:31]in.
Sleeve seam, 16½[17:17:17½: 18]in.
**Skirt.** Length, 19[19½:20:20½: 21]in.

| Gauge |
| --- |
| 6 sts and 8 rows to 1in over st st on No.4 needles. |

## Materials

Reynolds Tweed Courtelle
**Jacket.** 18[19:20:21:22] 40 grm balls
**Skirt.** 9[10:11:11:12] balls
One pair No. 3 needles (or Canadian No. 10)
One pair No. 4 needles (or Canadian No. 9)
8 buttons
One buckle
One 7 in skirt zipper
Waist length elastic for skirt

## Jacket back

Using No.3 needles, cast on 134[140:146:152:158] sts and K 10 rows.
Change to No.4 needles and continue in patt as follows:
**1st row** K.
**2nd row** P0[3:6:9:0], K2, *P10, K2, rep from *10[10:10 10:12] times more, P0[3:6:9:0]. These 2 rows form the patt and are rep throughout.
Continue in patt until work measures 2½in, ending with a WS row.
K2 tog at each end of next and every following 10th row until 104[110:116:122:128] sts rem.
Continue without shaping until work measures 22in from beg, ending with a WS row.

## Shape armholes

Bind off 9[10:11:11:12] sts at beg of next 2 rows, then 2sts

◄ *Garter stitch stripes in stockinette stitch create wide rib effect*

at beg of next 2 rows.
K2 tog at each end of every other row 4[4:4:5:5] times. 74[78:82:86:90] sts.
Continue without shaping until armhole measures 7[7½: 8:8½:9]in, ending with a WS row.

## Shape shoulders

Bind off 7[7:8:8:8] sts at beg of next 4 rows, then 7[8:7:8:9] sts at beg of next 2 rows.
Bind off rem 32[34:36:38:40] sts.

## Left front

Using No.3 needles, cast on 73[76:79:82:85] sts and K 10 rows.
Change to No.4 needles and continue in patt as follows:
**1st row** K.
**2nd row** K13, *P10, K2, rep from * 4[4:4:4:5] times, P0[3:6:9:0].
Rep the last 2 rows until work measures 2½in, ending with a WS row.
K2 tog at beg of next and every following 10th row until 58[61:64:67:70] sts rem.
Continue without shaping until work measures the same as Back to armholes, ending with a WS row.

## Shape armhole

At armhole edge, bind off 9[10:11:11:12] sts every other row; then 2 sts.
At arm edge, dec one st every other row 4[4:4:5:5] times. 43[45:47:49:51] sts.
Continue without shaping until armhole measures 4½[5: 5½:6:6]in, ending with a RS row.

## Shape neck

At neck edge, bind off 14[15:16: 17:18] sts, then 2 sts every other row 3 times.
K2 tog at neck edge every other row twice.
Continue without shaping until armhole measures the same as on Back, ending with a WS row.

## Shape shoulder

At arm edge, bind off 7[7:8: 8:8] sts every other row twice.

Work 1 row. Bind off rem 7[8:7:8:9] sts.
Mark position of buttons on front edge with pins as follows: Place first pin 2½in from beg, 2nd pin 3in below neck edge, then 6 more evenly spaced between these.

## Right front

Work to correspond to left Front, reversing all shaping and working buttonholes to correspond to pin positions as follows:
**Buttonhole row** (RS) K5, bind off 3 sts, patt to end.
**Next row** Cast on 3 sts over the 3 sts bound-off.

## Sleeves

Using No.3 needles, cast on 50[52:54:56:58] sts and K 10 rows.
Change to No.4 needles and continue in patt as follows:
**1st row** K.
**2nd row** P6[7:8:9:10], K2, *P10, K2, rep from * twice more, P6[7:8:9:10].
Continue in patt, inc one st at each end of every 8th row until there are 78[80:82:84:86] sts.
Continue without shaping until sleeve seam measures 16½[17:17:17½:18]in, ending with a WS row.

## Shape cap

Bind off 5 sts at beg of next 2 rows.
K2 tog at each end of every other row 15[16:17:18:19] times.
Bind off 2 sts at beg of next 12 rows.
Bind off rem 14 sts.

## Collar

Using No.3 needles, cast on 85[87:89:91:93] sts and work in garter st for 1¼in.
**Next row** K19[20:21:22:23], *K up 1, K2, K up 1, K3, rep from * 8 times more, K up 1, K2, K up 1, K19[20:21:22:23].
Continue in garter st for 2¾[2¾:3:3:3¼]in. Bind off.

## Belt

Using No.3 needles, cast on

11 sts. Work in garter st for 30[32:34:36:38]in. Bind off.

## Skirt front

Using No.3 needles, cast on 91[97:103:109:115] sts.
**1st row** K1, *P1, K1, rep from * to end.
**2nd row** P1, *K1, P1, rep from * to end.
Rep these 2 rows for 1½in, ending with a 2nd row.
Change to No.4 needles. Beg with a K row, work 4 rows st st.
**Next row** K10, K up 1, K24[26:28:30:32], K up 1, K23[25:27:29:31], K up 1, K24[26:28:30:32], K up 1, K10.
Work 5 rows.
**Next row** K10, *K up 1, K25[27:29:31:33], rep from * twice more, K up 1, K10.
Work 5 rows.
**Next row** K10, K up 1, K26[28:30:32:34], K up 1, K27[29:31:33:35], K up 1, K26[28:30:32:34], K up 1, K10.
Continue inc in this manner every 6th row twice more, then on every 10th row 9 times.
Continue without shaping until work measures 18[18½:19 19½:20]in from beg, ending with a K row.
Change to No.3 needles and K 10 rows. Bind off.

## Skirt back

Work as given for Front.

## Finishing

Press under a damp cloth and using a warm iron.

**Jacket**
Join shoulder seams.
Sew in Sleeves. Join side and sleeve seams. Sew on Collar. Press seams.
Sew on buttons. Make a loop on each side seam for belt, sew buckle to belt and thread through loops.

**Skirt.**
Join seams, leaving one open for zipper. Sew in zipper. Press seams. Sew elastic inside waistband with casing-stitch.

1747

# Crafts/making fabric boxes

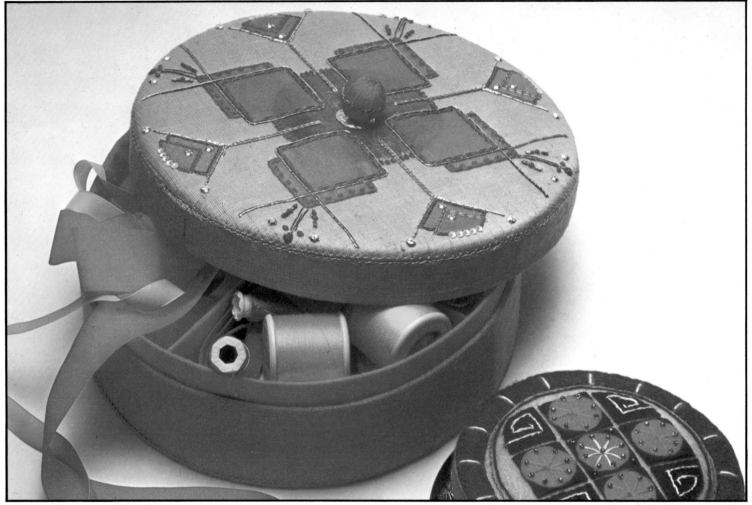

▲ *Make large boxes for sewing materials, jewelry, keepsakes; small boxes for pins and rings. Vary the fabric and decoration to suit yourself*

## The forgotten craft

Making embroidered fabric boxes is in some ways a forgotten craft. Many people, keen embroiderers, never think of turning their stitchcraft into the production of boxes—yet an exquisitely made fabric box provides the maker with a tremendous sense of achievement. Embroidered fabric boxes make marvelous gifts—but having made one you'll find it difficult to part with it.

Boxes take time, patience and care to make and measurements must be absolutely accurate if they are to look professional. Cleanliness is essential for this craft. Work with a clean cloth over your lap, and wash your hands frequently while working. Remember that adhesive dropped onto fabric will often leave a permanent mark and vigilance is needed during the glueing stages.

## Materials and equipment

Boxes are made of cardboard which is then padded and covered with fabric. Various weights of cardboard are used in box making and each of the projects in this chapter recommend the most suitable

weight of cardboard. Fabric adhesive is used for all glueing and it is best to use a narrow spatula for applying it.

Equipment needed for this craft is little more than you would need for any sewing craft, but you will also need a steel ruler, a good quality cutting knife, a set square and a piece of masonite for cutting on.

## Fabrics and padding

Thin smooth fabrics are better than thick ones, and those without excessive stretch in them are best. Silk, satin, rayon, linen, cotton, velvet and felt are all suitable fabrics, and those with lurex finishes or rich-looking prints make superb jewel boxes. The top of the box can be left plain if desired, or can be decorated with appliqué, beadwork, goldwork or surface embroidery of almost any kind to produce the desired effect.

Initials make boxes individual and beads can be piled one on another with sequins added for a jeweled effect. All surface embroidery must be completed before starting to construct the box. If patterned

fabrics are used, boxes often look prettier unadorned.

## Padding materials

The padding of the boxes which is placed immediately under the top fabric should be a plain fabric; cotton flannel or Pellon is recommended.

## Planning a box

First of all draw out the box you intend to make as a rough perspective drawing (diagram 1), and then draw out each piece, marking the measurements. Lining pieces are made smaller because you must allow for the thickness of padding and the covering material. Be very careful with these measurements if lids are to fit properly and not be too loose or fall into the edges of the box.

As you cut out each piece of cardboard, mark it clearly on the wrong side for outer, and right side for linings, so that you know which part of the box it is and whether it is a lining piece or outer piece. The mark is made because you will be covering one side of the cardboard with fabric, and

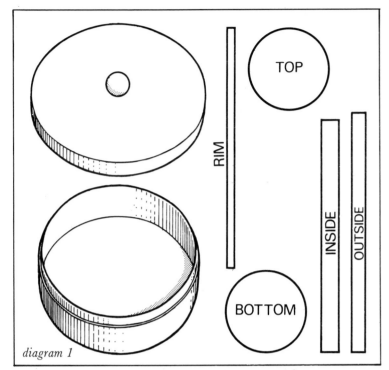

diagram 1

▲ *Rough perspective drawing of the box and opened up in sections*

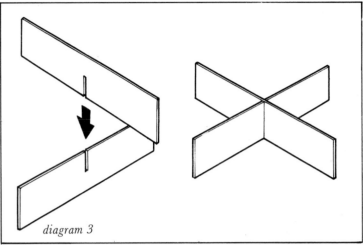

diagram 3

▲ *Making the dividing sections*

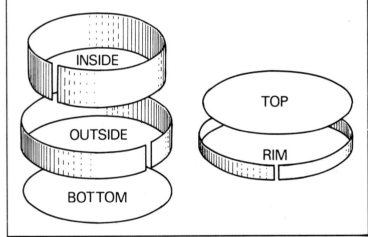

▲ *Drawing showing three sections of bottom of box*

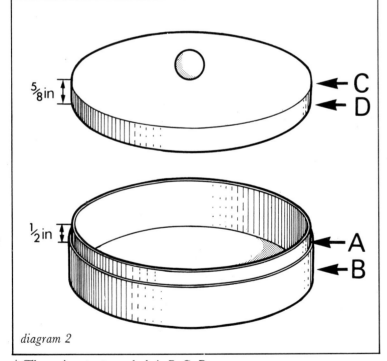

diagram 2

▲ *The various parts marked A, B, C, D*

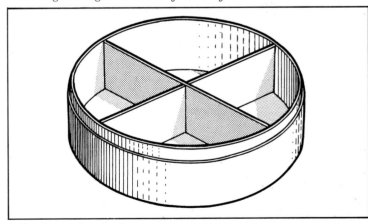

▲ *Showing sections in place*

pieces can easily lose their identity and become a bewildering muddle once you have begun to cover and pad.

# Round box with overlapping lid

Ticket-weight cardboard is used for the sides and the lining of the box. Mat board is used for the top and base. The outside measurement is just over 3 times (3.14) the diameter of the box bottom.

## Method

Cut the lining cardboard for the inside (marked A on diagram 2) so that it makes a circle $\frac{1}{2}$ inch deeper than the outer box side (marked B on diagram 2).

Form the lining and outer strips into circles by butting the ends and sticking the join with transparent tape (do not overlap joins because this causes a bump). Remember that when these two circles are fitted inside one another the joins must be kept apart or they form an ugly bump.

## Top

Cut out a circle from the mat board for the outside of the lid (C diagram 2). This should be exactly the diameter of the outside circle (B) just formed. Cut out the lining for the lid from the ticket-weight cardboard making it slightly smaller than the outside lid.

## Rim of lid

Cut this in ticket cardboard so that it makes a circle exactly the same circum-

▲ *Carefully planned abstract designs, worked in beads, sequins and thread on a plain fabric, can make an unusual decoration for a box lid*
▼ *Open Cretan stitch, used to stitch sections of fabric together*　　　　▼ *Mitering and snipping for lining and covering fabrics*

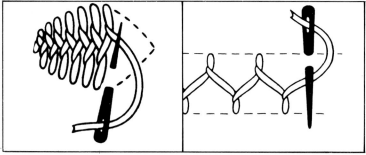

▼ *The method of construction for the felt box*

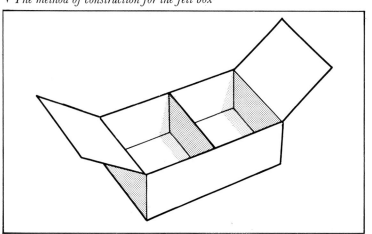

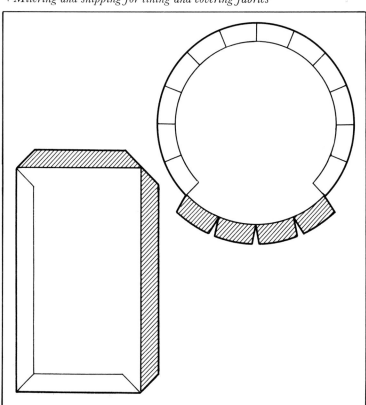

*▲ Richly embroidered fabrics, although expensive, make beautiful boxes. A small piece can be used to cover a little box for rings and brooches*

ference as the lid, and $\frac{5}{8}$ inch deep (D, diagram 2). Butt and join into a circle and stick with transparent tape.

### Bottom
Cut mat board to exactly the same diameter circle as the top and then cut the lining slightly smaller.

### Cutting the fabric
Cut fabrics for both outside of box and lining to the above sizes, allowing $\frac{1}{2}$ inch turnings. Allow $\frac{3}{4}$ inch extra when cutting the lining for (A) as it has to turn over the lip. Allow extra when cutting fabric for D as it has to turn under the rim.

### Padding
Cut padding to same size as the board.

### Applying padding
**Padding sides of box.** Glue two thicknesses of padding to the inside of the lining cardboard and to the outside of the outer cardboard, butting joins.
**Padding the bottom.** Cut two pieces of padding to the exact size of the bottom and two more pieces $\frac{1}{2}$ inch larger all

around. Using one same size and one larger size, glue the two thicknesses to the outside of the outer cardboard and two thicknesses to the inside of the lining cardboard. The bigger piece of padding is brought over the edge to round it off. Snip the edges for a smooth finish and glue down.
**Padding the top.** Glue two thicknesses of padding to the inside of the lining and at least three thicknesses of padding to the outside of the lid piece (C).

### Stages of covering the box
**Covering the sections. 1.** Join the side pieces of both outer and lining fabrics into a circle and press seams flat (A and B pieces).
**2.** Join rim fabric into a circle and press. Cover the side pieces A and B with fabric, glueing it into position and when completely dry, slip piece A into piece B.
**3.** Cover rim piece D with fabric, over sewing the open, upper edges together.
**4.** Cover the outside of the bottom circle and the inside of the lining circle with fabric, taking turnings over the edges.
**5.** Cover the top circle with fabric and decide at this point if a knob or top

decoration is desired. If so, stitch the knob to the circle, stitching right through the cardboard.
**6.** Stitch the rim to the top (along oversewn edge of rim) using open Cretan stitch and six strands of thread.
**7.** Join bottom circle to sides, using open Cretan stitch. When stitching pieces together, stitches should go through fabric and padding but not through the cardboard. Keep stitches regularly spaced.
**8.** Decide at this point if box divisions are desired (see diagram 3). Cover cardboard without padding it and then stitch the divisions to the bottom lining circle.
**9.** Put adhesive on the inside of the bottom circle and carefully press the lining section down upon it.
Put adhesive on the inside of the lid and press lining section onto it.
Leave to dry.

## Square boxes

Square boxes are made in exactly the same way as round boxes except that the four pieces of the lip and rim are sewn together at the joins.

# Stitchery design/pansy and anemone motifs

**Ways with flower motifs**

Motifs such as this simple pansy and anemone can be used for a wide variety of needlepoint items by enlarging or reducing them. Worked on large mesh canvas over more threads, they make squares for rugs or panels and pillows. Reduced, they can be used for curtain tie-back motifs and for stool tops. As petit point designs, they look pretty in miniature.

1752

Red flower square 12 inches by 11 inches
- ☐ 16in by 15in single-weave canvas with 10 threads to 1 inch
- ☐ Matte embroidery cotton in orange, red, white and green
- ☐ D.M.C. Pearl Cotton No.1 in scarlet

Purple flower square 12in by 13in
- ☐ 16in by 17in single-weave canvas with 10 threads to 1 inch
- ☐ Matte embroidery cotton in silver gray, purple, and white

- ☐ D.M.C. Pearl Cotton No.1 in bright pink and purple

**To work the squares**

Mark the center of the rectangle of canvas each way with lines of basting stitches. Work in cross-stitch over two threads of canvas each way, following the designs from the center of charts.

If both designs are to be incorporated in a piece of work, extend the background of the red flower to match the purple.

*Floral motifs enlarged to make a rug, reduced to ornament a box lid, and used same size for a stool*

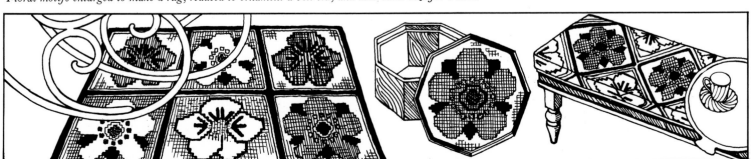

# Stitchery pattern/tablecloth in blackwork

This striking tablecloth in blackwork combines backstitch, cross-stitch and whipped backstitch. It is worked here on pale blue linen, but would be equally attractive on a white or strongly contrasting background.

To make this tablecloth you will need:
- ☐ 1⅝ yds 59 inch wide pale blue even-weave embroidery linen
- ☐ D.M.C. Pearl Cotton No.8, 5 balls black 0403
- ☐ Tapestry needle No.24

**Method**

Square the fabric and mark the center each way with lines of basting stitches. The photograph on the facing page gives one quarter of the design. The center is the upper left-hand corner of the photograph, and this should coincide with the basting stitches on the fabric. The number within the bracket indicates the number of threads between the center section of the design and the border. Note also from the photograph the arrangement of the stitches on the threads of the fabric. Commence the embroidery at the top of each central flower motif, 36 threads down from the crossed basting stitches, and work the center section and border section as given. Repeat in reverse from the left-hand edge of the photograph to complete one half of the design. Then turn the fabric and work the other half in the same way.

Press the embroidery on the wrong side. To finish, turn back a one inch hem on all the edges, miter the corners and then slip stitch.

center

120

Border
repeats
from here

1755

# Tailoring seven

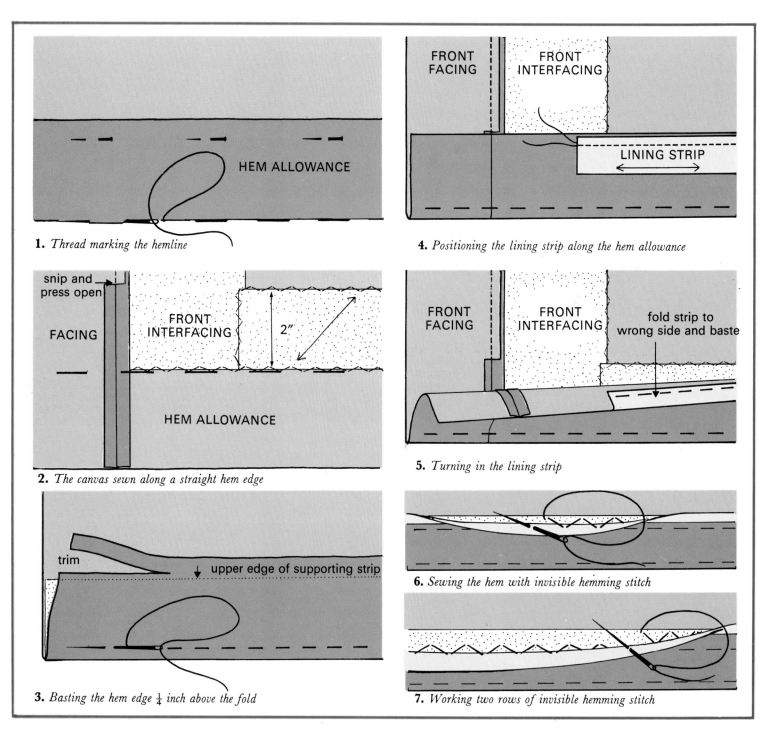

**1.** *Thread marking the hemline*

**4.** *Positioning the lining strip along the hem allowance*

FRONT FACING

FRONT INTERFACING

LINING STRIP

snip and press open

FACING

FRONT INTERFACING

2"

HEM ALLOWANCE

**2.** *The canvas sewn along a straight hem edge*

FRONT FACING

FRONT INTERFACING

fold strip to wrong side and baste

**5.** *Turning in the lining strip*

trim

upper edge of supporting strip

**3.** *Basting the hem edge ¼ inch above the fold*

**6.** *Sewing the hem with invisible hemming stitch*

**7.** *Working two rows of invisible hemming stitch*

**A. Sewing the hem:** straight hem; curved hem.
**B. Finishing the facing**
**C. Finishing piped buttonholes**
**D. Hand-worked buttonholes:** sham buttonholes.
**E. The final press**
**F. Sewing on the buttons:** making a shank; keeper button.
**\*Terms and stitches**

## A. Sewing the hem

### Straight hem

These instructions are for a coat which

has a perfectly straight hem edge or is only very slightly curved.
**1.** Thread mark the fold of the hem then remove the pins.
**2.** To give the hem a good crisp finish, support the hem edge with strips of duck or canvas. Cut the strips 2 inches wide on the bias of the fabric and to the length of the coat hem edge, joining if necessary to make up the required length. Sew to the hem edge with catch stitch as shown.
**3.** Turn up the hem and baste flat ¼ inch above the fold. Press well, making sure that the iron does not impress the hem edge into the fabric.

Measure the hem depth to just above the supporting strips and trim.
To bind the seam allowance on the hem, cut 1 inch wide strips of coat lining fabric on the straight of grain. The selvage is useful for this.
**4.** Position the lining strip on the hem edge, but, to avoid bulk, do not continue the binding along the part of the hem which will be under the front facings. Stitch, taking ¼ inch seam allowance.
**5.** Fold the binding to the wrong side and baste. Press, making sure the hem lies away from the coat, otherwise impressions will be left on the coat fabric.
**6.** Baste the hem in place matching seams.

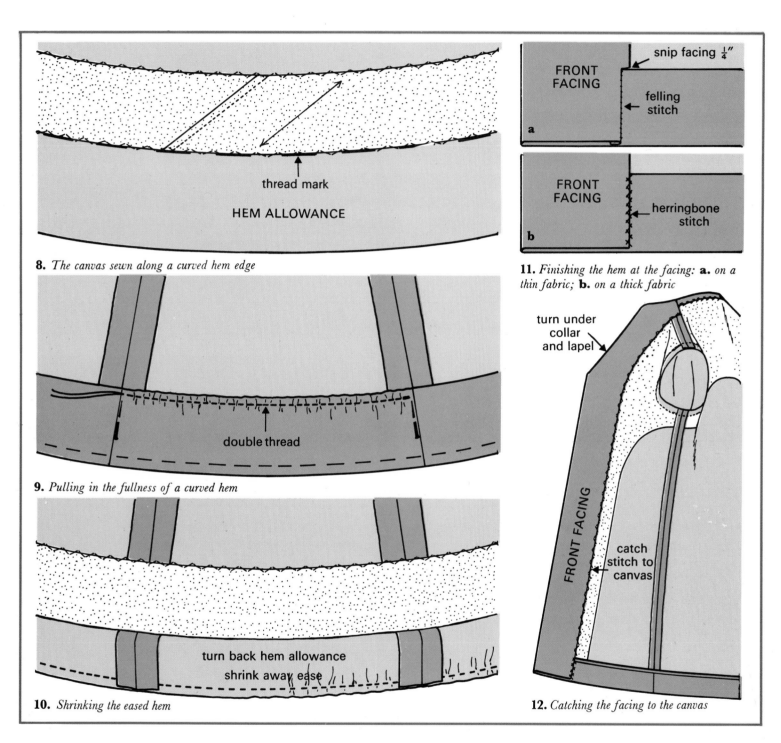

**8.** *The canvas sewn along a curved hem edge*

**9.** *Pulling in the fullness of a curved hem*

**10.** *Shrinking the eased hem*

**11.** *Finishing the hem at the facing:* **a.** *on a thin fabric;* **b.** *on a thick fabric*

**12.** *Catching the facing to the canvas*

Then, with the folded hem edge toward you, lift the hem slightly and sew neatly to the canvas with invisible hemming stitch*.

**7.** If the coat is very heavy, or you have left a deep hem as on a child's coat, sew two lines of invisible hemming stitch to hold the weight.

**Curved hem**

For a coat with a flare use this method of putting up the hem.

**8.** First work as for a straight hem edge in figures 1 and 2, gently easing the canvas into position around the curve of the coat hem.

Turn the hem up and baste flat ¼ inch above the fold, then trim the hem edge to just above the supporting strips as for the straight hem (figure **3**).

**9.** Matching center backs and fronts and seamlines, pin the hem as shown. Then run a double thread through each section, pulling up the fullness until the hem lies flat.

**10.** Lift the hem away from the coat and shrink away the ease.

To bind the seam allowance on the hem, cut 1 inch wide strips of coat lining fabric on the bias, then continue binding and sewing up the hem as for the straight hem as shown in figures **4**, **5**, **6** and **7**.

## B. Finishing the facing

Place the coat on a flat surface and turn the facing to the inside. There are two ways of finishing off the hem edge.

**11a, b.** On thin fabrics, first snip into the facing seam allowance at the top of the hem. Then turn the facing under ¼ inch at the hem edge and fell firmly in place to the hem seam allowance (**a**). On thick fabrics do not turn under the raw edge to make neat, but simply herringbone the raw edge in position (**b**).

**12.** To finish off the facing, lay the coat flat, facing side up and lapel turned under. Catch stitch the facing to the canvas.

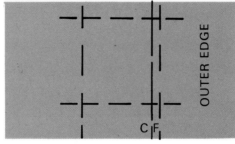

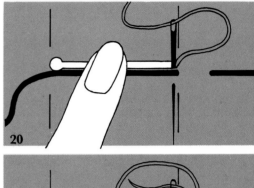

**15.** *Tram lines for hand-worked buttonholes*

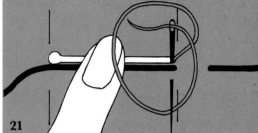

**16.** *The outer edge of the hand-worked buttonhole:* **a.** *circle;* **b.** *a triangle*

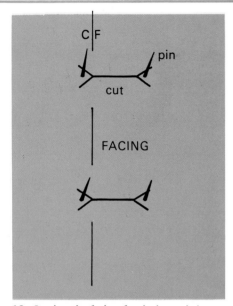

**13.** *Cutting the facing for the buttonholes*

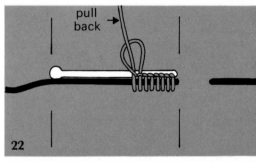

**17.** *The cut buttonhole*

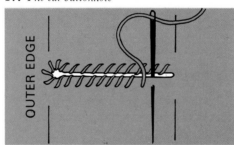

**18.** *Oversewing the buttonhole with single thread*

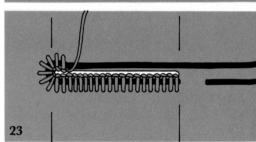

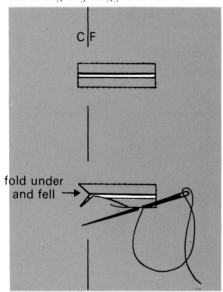

**14.** *Finishing the back of the buttonhole*

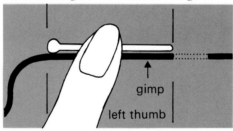

**19.** *Gimp laid along the buttonhole*

**20 to 23.** *Working the buttonhole*

## C. Finishing piped buttonholes

With the facing now in its final position it is time to finish the back of the piped buttonholes.

Working from the right side, push a pin through to the wrong side at each end of the buttonhole to find the exact position of the slit on the facing.

**13.** Make a slit through the facing between the pins and miter the corners just beyond the pins.

**14.** Fold under the raw edges and fell securely in place.

Finally, press on the wrong side.

## D. Hand-worked buttonholes

Tailored, hand-worked buttonholes are
1758

beautiful when sewn evenly, so practice on a double piece of the fabric with interfacing in between before starting on the garment itself.

The thread used is silk buttonhole twist and you will also need buttonhole gimp. An alternative to buttonhole gimp is two threads of buttonhole twist waxed together to prevent them from untwisting.

**15.** Prepare the buttonhole tram lines (see also Tailoring 3, figure 10, page 1676).

**16a, b.** Using a stiletto, make a round hole at the outer edge of the buttonhole (**a**), or cut out a triangle (**b**).

**17.** Continuing from the hole, cut the length of the buttonhole. Cut very carefully as a jagged line shows up on the finished buttonhole.

**18.** Using a single strand of matching thread, oversew around the buttonhole

through all thicknesses.

**19.** Lay the gimp along the buttonhole as shown. The gimp is held in place with the thumb when working the buttonhole.

Thread the needle with a long length of buttonhole twist so that you will have enough to finish the buttonhole without joining.

**20.** Starting at the point shown and working with the right side of the coat facing you, insert the needle through the back of the buttonhole making sure that all layers of the fabric are caught.

**21.** Take the thread forward under the needle.

**22.** Pull the needle through and tighten the loop with the thread pulled back, so that the knot lies on the cut edge of the buttonhole.

**23.** At the circle or triangle, fan the stitches

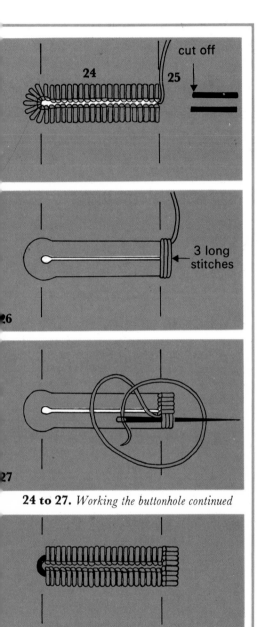

**24 to 27.** *Working the buttonhole continued*

**28.** *A sham buttonhole*

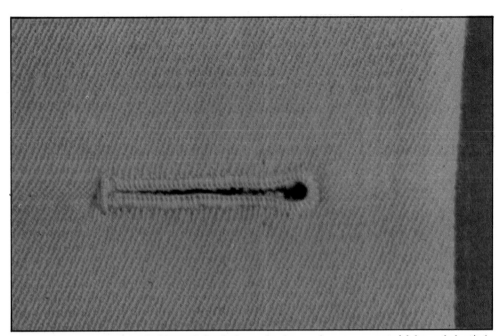

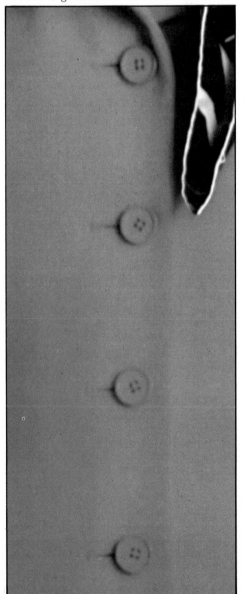

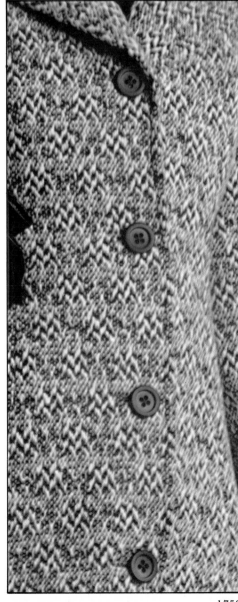

**Above:** *Enlarged hand-worked buttonhole; the button bar has not been sewn over with buttonhole stitch.*
**Below:** *A garment with hand-worked buttonholes (left) and a garment with piped buttonholes (right)*

out wider at the outer edge of the curve.

**24.** Complete the other side of the buttonhole but do not cut off the thread yet.

**25.** Pull the gimp tight, thread between the layers of fabric and cut off.

**26.** To make the bar tack at the end of the buttonhole, work three long stitches as shown for the bar.

**27.** Work buttonhole stitch over the bar and through the fabric, bringing the knots to the top as shown.

### Sham buttonholes

Sham buttonholes are sometimes made for vents.

**28.** Without cutting a slit, work buttonhole stitch along the buttonhole line. Make a bar tack at the end but omit the circle at the front end, as the button covers the lack of circle.

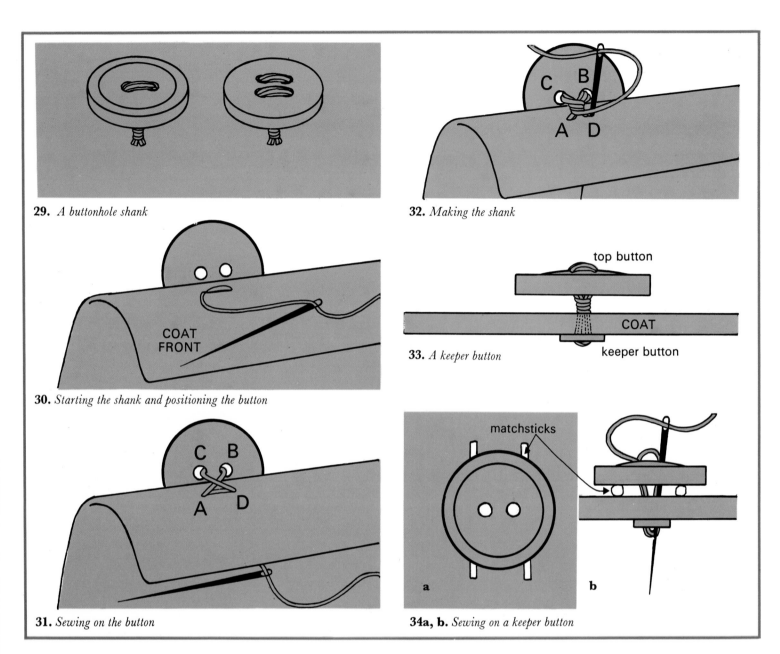

**29.** *A buttonhole shank*

**32.** *Making the shank*

**30.** *Starting the shank and positioning the button*

COAT FRONT

**33.** *A keeper button*

top button

COAT

keeper button

**31.** *Sewing on the button*

C B
A D

**34a, b.** *Sewing on a keeper button*

matchsticks

a

b

# E. The final pressing

Lay the coat right side up on a board.
Using a wool pressing cloth under a slightly damp cotton cloth, gently press all over the coat, moving each section of the coat so that it lies flat as you press it.
This process should be done with hardly any pressure on the iron to avoid making impressions on the coat.
Hang the coat to dry before lining.

# F. Sewing on the buttons

Before the coat is lined the buttons should be sewn on.

### Making a shank
**29.** A flat button should be sewn on with a shank so that the button does not distort the buttonhole by being too close to the fabric.

**30.** Using a strong buttonhole thread, take a backstitch through the fabric at the button position. Do not use a knot.
Fold the coat back and hold the button in position as shown.
**31.** Take thread from A through holes B, and then C, then back into fabric at D. Repeat three or four times, and again if the button has four holes. This gives crossed threads which make a strong foundation for the shank.
**32.** With the thread coming out from C, wind it tightly around the shank. Take the thread to the back and fasten off securely to finish.

### Keeper button
**33.** For added strength, a little keeper button can be sewn onto the back of the coat at the same time as the top button is being sewn on.
The keeper button should be a tiny but-

ton with the same number of holes as the top button.
**34a, b.** Lay the top button over two matchsticks (**a**) and sew on the button, at the same time sewing through the matching holes on the keeper button (**b**). Leave the thread quite loose.
Remove the matchsticks and make a shank (see figure 32).

# *Terms and stitches

### Invisible hemming stitch (35)

**35**